Onkle
Henry a
Sat darg

PRISONER OF

HOPE

W - 360 - 5184494
H - 360 - 7183281

Captivated by the
Expectation of Good

Randi —
Hope is chasing
you, surrounding you
and flowing through you —
Blessings!
David
Eph 3:20

PRISONER OF
HOPE

Captivated by the Expectation of Good

David Crone

Published by:
NIS VENTURES INTERNATIONAL
6391 Leisure Town Road, Vacaville, California 95687

Cover and interior paintings by Deborah Crone
Graphic Design by Ron Cantrell

Printed in the United States of America

Dedication

This book is dedicated to our daughter, Amy Sue, whose sudden journey to Heaven compelled us to explore the true value of hope.

Acknowledgments

I want to express my deep appreciation for the friends and co-laborers at The Mission who have journeyed with Deborah and me and whose prayers and encouragement sustained us in difficult times.

I cannot fail to acknowledge Ivan Tait, a friend who moved aside his own busy life and came to our home during the most painful week of our lives. He was, to us and our family, Holy Spirit in the flesh.

Most of all, I wish to express my love and gratitude to my parents for their prayers and encouragement; to my sons and their wives for their constant love and support; and to Deborah, my childhood friend who became my lifelong companion, for her unfailing courage and inspiration.

Endorsements

David Crone's powerful new book, *Prisoner of Hope*, is more than a book; it's a Holy Spirit roadmap into freedom and power. Countless people are imprisoned by life-controlling anxiety attacks and mind-numbing fear. This book reveals the strategies on how to escape the grasp of the enemy and win the battle against hopelessness. If you are held hostage by the fear of failure, despair, or depression, this book will help you break free from the chains that hold you captive and win the victory against fear. Get ready to unlock divine opportunities and be released into your destiny. I highly recommend this book!

—KRIS VALLOTTON
Leader, Bethel Church, Redding, California
Co-Founder of Bethel School of Supernatural Ministry
Author of ten books including, *The Supernatural Ways of Royalty* and *Spirit Wars*

David Crone is a skillful writer and has penned a masterpiece of hope. In *Prisoner of Hope: Captivated by the Expectation of Good,* David has gone into the heart of God and brought out hope gold. Every page is full of fresh inspiration and transforming truth. *Prisoner of Hope* is the best book on hope I have ever read. Its only negative is that it is too short. I could have read another 50 chapters!

—IVAN TAIT
Founder and CEO of What Matters Ministries and Missions
Author of *Letters From God*

The ultimate weight of an author's words emerges from the depth of his character and experiences. I know of no truer prisoner of hope than David Crone. In this book, David blazes for us a tear-stained, hope-filled trail through the darkest valleys of the shadow of death. David's personal insights and revelations give us right, might, and reason to choose hope above all circumstance, to disarm the powers of despair, and to stare boldly and triumphantly into the face of life's greatest adversities and determine in our heart-of-hearts to truly live.

—DAN MCCOLLAM
Founding director of Sounds of the Nations, Mission School of Worship, and Mission School of Prophecy
Author of *God Vibrations, Basic Training For Prophetic Activation* and the children's series, *My Super Powers*

Contents

Return to the stronghold,
you prisoners of hope; even today I declare
that I will restore double to you.

—Zechariah 9:12, emphasis added

Introduction

THIS BOOK IS NOT BUSINESS . . . it's personal. It is not another book about the subject of ministry or even another self-help book. My intent of writing *Prisoner of Hope: Captivated By the Expectation of Good* is to communicate a very personal journey in order to help you, the reader, on your own. Deborah and I have explored the subject of hope from the inside out until it is no longer theory but a living reality. In fact, the last several years of our lives as a couple and as a family could make for a riveting, dramatic, event-filled TV reality show. It is doubtful, though, that many would believe it to be true. However, our story believed or not, I think we can all agree that we live in a time when hope is being consistently and brutally assaulted.

13

PRISONER OF HOPE

The Hebrews who lived following the seventy years of captivity in Babylon would have had no trouble believing it; they were living their own kind of reality show. I imagine the excitement and joy of returning to their homeland became a fading memory in light of the overwhelming responsibility of all the renovation needed to restore their nation back to its former glory. The Israelites were reeling under a confused identity, having resided their entire lives as captives in a foreign land. The earthly residence of their God stood only half completed for more than a dozen years as the enemies of Israel derided their progress. Hope was definitely under attack.

It was in this storm of political turmoil, and social and religious malaise, that the prophet Zachariah emerged to speak to God's people. The prophet, whose name means "God remembers," told Israel about a new season based upon the blood covenant (a covenant God had not forgotten about) that was now upon them.

> *As for you also, because of the blood of your covenant, I will set your prisoners free from the waterless pit. Return to the stronghold, you prisoners of hope. Even today I declare that I will restore double to you* (Zechariah 9:11-12).

What catches my attention in these two verses is Zechariah's description of two types of prisoners. The first mentioned are those who are imprisoned in a "waterless pit," unable to escape their circumstances and filled with despair. The good news for these prisoners was that God remembered them, and they would be set free.

The second group of prisoners mentioned is the one that interests me most. Zechariah calls them "prisoners of hope"—those who have chosen not to live as prisoners of despair, but who choose to be captivated by the expectation of good coming their way. They are the ones who maintain an expectation from a good God who does not forget His promises. These prisoners are caught in the grips of hope—a hope that is found in the stronghold of the God of all hope.

One of the movies I enjoy watching over and over is, "Elizabeth: The Golden Age." It chronicles the early years of Queen Elizabeth I in her rule of England up to the destruction of the Spanish Armada. I enjoy the movie for at least two reasons. First of all, the historical context feeds my love of history. Second, the film's attraction for me is a mesmerizing scene between Sir Walter Raleigh and Queen Elizabeth.

This scene begins with the queen's inquiry into Raleigh's exploits on the high seas. As he describes his experience of sailing from England in search of the New World, the word pictures Raleigh draws for her seem to hypnotize Queen Elizabeth. It is at this point in the movie that I nearly stop breathing, not wanting any sound to cause me to miss one single word of Raleigh's narrative spoken in a near whisper.

The following is his description.

Can you imagine what it is to cross an ocean? For weeks you see nothing but the horizon, perfect and empty. You live in the grip of fear: fear of storms, fear of sickness on board, fear of the immensity. So you must drive that fear down deep into your belly, study your charts, watch your compass, pray for a fair wind, and hope—pure, naked, fragile hope.

15

PRISONER OF HOPE

At first it's no more than a haze on the horizon, so you watch. You watch, and there's a smudge—a shadow—on the far water. For a day, for another day, a stain slowly spreads along the horizon taking form until on the third day you let yourself believe. You dare to whisper the word, "land." Land: life, resurrection, a true adventure coming out of the vast unknown, out of the immensity into new life. That, your Majesty, is the New World.[1]

I have watched this film more than ten times and every time the impact is the same—total captivation at the words, "So you must drive that fear down deep into your belly, study your charts, watch your compass, pray for a fair wind, and hope—pure, naked, fragile hope."

There have been times at the conclusion of that scene that I've heard myself whisper (as if responding to Raleigh), "I know what you mean."

And I do. Deborah and I know what it is to be living in the whirlwind of challenging, gut-wrenching, and sometimes tragic circumstances assaulting our soul, being held on course by a seemingly fragile, yet intensely tenacious embrace of hope. We know what it is like to be a "prisoner of hope."

As I began to write this part of the Introduction I thought it would be helpful for you to have some idea of what those storms that we have traveled through in the last six years looked like. Then I thought again. After typing out some of the opposing circumstances and reading them off the computer screen, I realized that to list them here for you would be doing what I had promised myself never to do—keep track of the cost. Though, in this book, I will refer to some of our experiences, they will only be used to open windows of revelation, exposing the life-giving power of hope anchored in a good God.

It was also clear to me in typing out the list that these "light and momentary troubles"[2] as Paul calls them, do not reflect in any way the amazing life of hope we have lived in the midst of every storm that threw itself against us. Though we can personally relate to David's cry, "I would have lost heart, unless I had believed that I would see the goodness of the Lord in the land of the living,"[3] we equally relate to, and wholeheartedly embrace, Paul's declaration:

> *For our light and momentary troubles are achieving for us an eternal glory that far outweighs them all* (2 Corinthians 4:17, NIV).

It is my desire that as you read *Prisoner of Hope: Captivated By the Expectation of Good,* you, too, will find yourself increasingly captivated by hope and overcome by the goodness of God. Both His hope and His goodness are made for these times that we live in. They are specifically intended for seasons of hopelessness. God's goodness and His hope shine brightest in the dark times and prove their greatest strength in the days of our weakness.

Please join me, as ones who live with the God of all hope resident in our being, and plunge into the privilege of living as a prisoner of hope.

Endnotes

1. "Elizabeth, The Golden Age," University Pictures and Working Title Films, 2007.
2. See 2 Cor. 4:17.
3. Ps. 27:13.

Let your hopes,
not your hurts, shape your future.

—Robert H. Schuller

CHAPTER ONE

Living in

Context

AFTER NEARLY FORTY YEARS OF full-time vocational ministry, the leadership at The Mission generously released us for a three-month sabbatical. We spent the first month enjoying the sun and sand on the beautiful island of Maui, Hawaii.

Never having been on a sabbatical, I wasn't sure what to expect, but I was hoping it would be a time of fresh revelation from Holy Spirit. I went to sleep the first night in Maui with that longing expressed in my sighing prayer. When I awoke the next morning I was not disappointed as Holy Spirit downloaded into my spirit a revelation on the importance of "context."

Slipping quietly out of bed before dawn so as not to awaken Deb, I went to the lanai, opened my laptop, and began to record the thoughts that were so newly revelatory to me. My excitement rose as the thought came to me: every morning is going to be like this one—full of fresh downloads of truth! What actually happened on each of the following mornings, however, was not at all like that first dawn. In fact, I did not have another morning like that one during the entire sabbatical!

Nevertheless, what I did experience was a life-changing journey with Holy Spirit exploring the power, impact, and value of context and its importance in understanding this thing called hope. Allow me to share with you some of the insights gained through that journey.

Historical or Personal

Several years ago, Deborah and I enjoyed a trip throughout England, Wales, and Scotland. One of the highlights of the trip was our time spent in the beautiful historic city of Edinburgh, Scotland. Dominating the city's skyline from its position atop the volcanic Castle Rock sits the centuries old Edinburgh Castle.

Within the ancient walls of the castle you will find Crown Square, also known as Palace Yard. On the north end of Crown Square, there is a converted barracks that now houses the Scottish National War Memorial. It was established to commemorate the Scottish soldiers who gave their lives in both world wars and several following military conflicts. This part of the castle was of special interest to me as a history buff, particularly of World War II history.

Just before entering the memorial, I noticed a park bench with a plaque that read:

Living in Context

When you return, tell them of us and say, "For your tomorrows, we have given our todays."

I found myself immediately sobered by the hollowed ground I was about to walk on.

It would be very difficult for me to try to adequately describe the memorial, so I will do so very simply. You enter into a large rotunda with high stone walls and well-worn stone floors. On the far side, opposite the entrance, is a partitioned area designated as a shrine to the unknown soldiers—those whose bodies were found on the battlefield but could not be identified by name.

As we entered the memorial, we were surprised to hear the sound of women chatting rather loudly and a group of men laughing over something they found humorous. Their demeanor seemed out of place to us, lacking the honor due the men and women who had given the ultimate sacrifice for their country.

As we were contemplating the rudeness of their actions, a stately, gray-haired man who looked to be in his seventies or eighties caught our attention as he entered the rotunda. The man, dressed in civilian clothing yet with a soldier's bearing, walked across the floor and stood at attention before the shrine. None of the others present nor the inappropriate chatter inside the memorial seemed to distract him at all. He stood erect, staring straight ahead in complete silence—fully focused on the tomb of the Unknown Soldier. Soon, tears began to run down the man's cheeks, yet he made no move to wipe them away. After what must have been no more than a minute or so, the elderly gentleman saluted sharply, turned in military fashion, and marched out of the memorial.

We were mesmerized by this moving display we had just witnessed. We stood there speechless; words could not adequately describe our emotions at that moment, and silence was the only honorable response. Yet, during the entire experience, the group of ladies never stopped their chatter, and the men continued to berate the atmosphere with frivolity.

I was fascinated by the contrast and wondered what explained the difference in response. How could one person stand in this place of honor without honor, while another enters with respect and demonstrates his highest tribute? And then it came to me: to the one it was an event of history; to the other it was personal. Context.

The Hot Dog Stand

Imagine with me the following scenario: two men approach a hot dog vendor at mid-day in downtown New York City. The placard on the side of the cart reads, "Hot Dogs: $3.95." The first man walks to the stand with confidence and directs the vendor to make him a "foot-long with all the trimmings." He reaches into the pocket of his designer suit and hands the vendor a five-dollar bill and casually says, "Keep the change." He walks away eating his hot dog, being careful not to drip anything on his tailored suit. After a few bites, the man remembers he is scheduled to have a late lunch with his wife and, not wanting to spoil his appetite, tosses the remainder of his meal into the trash.

The second man stands at a distance from the hot dog cart for few minutes as if evaluating his choice. Eventually, he steps toward the stand and cautiously inquires if the trimmings are included with the hot dog for the $3.95 price. After learning that they are, he orders his foot-long dog and pulls out a few bills, along with some loose change, from his worn, tattered coat. He counts the money very carefully and hands the vendor the exact change. Upon receiving his prize, he moves to a bench and sits down to eat it. He chews slowly, savoring every bite, and when there is a little less than half left, he carefully wraps the remainder and tucks it in the inside pocket of his jacket.

The difference in the approach of two men to the same hot dog stand is context. The first man has a $140,000 annual salary, a fairly large bank account, and a fully vested retirement plan. He ate at a high-end bistro the night before, slept soundly in his bed beneath luxurious imported cotton sheets, and woke to a hot breakfast. He approached the vendor with $125 cash in his wallet.

The second man has been several months without an income. He exhausted his bank account weeks ago, and his retirement plan never existed. He ate what was left of a can of soup the night before and slept fitfully between thread-bare sheets on the lumpy bed of the hotel room where he has lived since losing his house. He ate no breakfast that morning, and he approached the vendor with only $5.74 to his name.

These two men stand in two totally different contexts which determine the way they each look at that $3.95 hot dog. One sees it as a snack, the other as possibly his last meal. One buys on an impulse, the other buys in order to survive. One wonders about the quality, the other wonders if he can find it cheaper down the street.

The context of our individual lives is a huge influencer of the way we see and respond to life and the world around us. A bus driver approaches a narrow city street far differently than the driver of a smart car. A man in a wheelchair sees a set of stairs differently than a man out for a morning walk. The woman who had been physically abused as a child may respond distrustingly to the touch of a man, unlike another woman who had been tenderly nurtured and loved into adulthood.

Real and Perceived

Have you ever wondered why you were so confident in one setting yet lacking in confidence in another? It is context—both real and perceived.

One day, when Deborah and I were first part of the church that is now The Mission, I had to drive from Vacaville to Sacramento to visit a friend in the hospital. The car I was driving at the time was less than pristine in its condition. It had one tire that particularly needed to be replaced. I was confident that it ran well enough to transport me safely the 35-miles there and back. *Besides* (convincing myself), *I have a very good spare in the trunk, and I'm certainly familiar with changing tires.*

Context can be the difference between dreams realized or dreams abandoned.

On the way to the hospital, I never gave the vehicle or its safety another thought. I drove my usual speed, put a cassette in the tape player, turned up the volume, and just enjoyed the ride. I arrived at the hospital and had a wonderful visit with my friend. When I pulled onto the freeway to head back to Vacaville, I suddenly remembered that just the day before I had taken the spare tire out of the car to vacuum the trunk and had not put it back! I quickly responded to this revelation by turning off the music so I could listen instead to the sounds of the vehicle, nearly panicking with every odd noise I heard. I slowed the speed of the vehicle to several miles an hour under the speed limit and became acutely aware of all my surroundings. The trip that had been so relaxing and enjoyable up to this

24

point was now filled with high stress and great concern. My perceived context had changed into an actual context.

Context affects our decisions. It limits or expands our perspective. It even defines for us what we see as possibilities and influences the very quality of our lives. The result can be living in fear of impending crises or living with hopeful expectancy. It can be the difference between dreams realized or dreams abandoned, defeat or victory.

What About Choice?

The question that begs asking is this: are we simply victims of a context we can do nothing about, or can we choose the context we live from?

When the young shepherd boy, David, stepped alone into the valley between the armies of Israel and the Philistines, he was entering a context of intimidation, threat, and defeat. Twice a day for the previous forty days, the Israeli soldiers would shine their armor, sharpen their swords, and parade out in battle array before the Philistine army. Once set in their battle lines, they would shout their war cry and await the response of their enemy.

Each time it was the same: the Philistine giant, Goliath, would step out cloaked in his massive armor, ridicule Israel and her God, and then challenge any Israelite to come and fight him—one-on-one. It was at this point that the army of Israel turned in panic and ran screaming back to the safety of their tents.

Enter David. He knew that 79 times the "army of the Living God" had retreated in fear from Goliath. He knew that not one of the mighty warriors of Israel was willing to take on this imposing giant. The smell of intimidation and shame must have been thick in the atmosphere.

Yet, when David stood before the mighty Philistine, he responded with confidence and courage.

> *You come to me with sword, with a spear, and with a javelin. But I come to you in the name of the LORD of hosts, the God of the armies of Israel, whom you have defied. This day the LORD will deliver you into my hand... And this day I will give the carcasses of the camp of the Philistines to the birds of the air... Then all this assembly shall know that the LORD does not save with sword and spear; for the battle is the LORD'S, and He will give you into our hands* (I Samuel 17:45-47).

David chose his context. Instead of fighting from the caustic atmosphere of the present circumstances, David chose to fight from the context of his history in God. Listen to his declaration to King Saul:

> *Your servant used to keep his father's sheep, and when a lion or a bear came and took a lamb out of the flock, I went out after it and struck it, and delivered the lamb from its mouth; and when it arose against me, I caught it by its beard, and struck and killed it. Your servant has killed both lion and bear; and this uncircumcised Philistine will be like one of them, seeing he has defied the armies of the living God* (vs. 34-36).

We see the option to choose context throughout Scripture. Most of the great stories in the Bible that we studied in Sunday school are stories of men and women choosing to live, fight, or worship from a context different

Living in Context

from their surroundings or circumstances. Often their chosen context stood in direct opposition to the thoughts, feelings, and opinions of those around them. Consider, for instance, the three Hebrew young men entering the fiery furnace; Daniel walking into the lion's den; Esther approaching the king upon threat of her life; Gideon taking on the enemy numbering 135,000 with an army of 300 men equipped only with horns, sticks, and vases; Caleb and Joshua standing in the face of a negative report and declaring that the giants of the land were theirs for the taking.

Each of these stories, and many others, tell of those who refused to allow the circumstances of their lives, the conditions of their situations, or the voices of opposition, to dictate their contexts. If they could choose, so can we.

As for me and my house, we choose the context of His presence—the place where hope lives.

To live without hope is to cease to live.

—Fyodor Dostoevsky

CHAPTER TWO

His Presence,

Our Natural Home

THE SPORT OF SCUBA HAS BECOME ONE of life's great pleasures for me. Descending beneath the surface of the ocean, I enter an environment otherwise off limits to us oxygen-breathing creatures. It's not that I get to stop breathing O^2. Rather, I take it with me—strapped to my back, compressed in a metal cylinder, and fed through a hose attached to a regulator. Through this marvelous apparatus, I escape into the glorious world of beautiful coral and colorful fish where the only sound is my own rhythmic inhaling and exhaling of life-giving oxygen.

The first time I tried SCUBA, it was not such a glorious event. In fact, it was terrifying. My initiation into the sport took place in the warm waters off the coast of Maui in the crater of the small island of Molikini. On the way out to the dive spot, I received fifteen minutes of instruction on the use of the equipment along with its unique terminology and protocol.

"The number one rule of diving," the instructor declared, "is to breathe!" With that injunction, my diving education was complete, and I was confident that I was now competent enough to dive—or so I believed.

When we arrived at the dive spot, I strapped on my BCD (short for Buoyancy Compensator Device) which held the oxygen tank to my back and allowed me to regulate my depth. I then put on the weight belt prescribed by the dive master that allowed me to sink into the water, slipped on my fins, tested the regulator to make sure it was dispensing the oxygen properly, put the mask over my face, and enthusiastically jumped into the ocean. Upon hitting the water, I inflated my BCD as instructed and waited for the dive master to give the signal to dive. I was very excited.

God's Presence is our natural habitat, our authentic context for life.

There was no horn sounding or anyone yelling, "Dive! Dive!"—just a simple thumbs down signal by the dive master. With the regulator firmly clenched between my teeth, I released the air from my BCD and slipped below the surface of the water. Within 20-seconds and 10-feet of descent, I raced to the surface as quickly as my fins could propel me, convinced that if I remained submerged I was going to die from lack of oxygen.

The instructor noticed my rapid ascent and joined me on the surface.

"My regulator is not working!" I informed him breathlessly. After testing it, he handed it back to me and stated, "It's working just fine."

"But, I wasn't getting any oxygen! I couldn't breathe," I emphatically declared.

"You were getting all the oxygen you needed," he calmly informed me. "The problem," he continued, "is that your mind is telling you it is not natural to breathe underwater, and you're believing it. Try again, and this time ignore what your mind is telling you. Instead, trust your equipment and remember the number one rule: breathe."

I did try it again, and for several terrifying minutes I frantically fought panic, sucking air as fast as I could, forgetting at times to exhale. It wasn't until I began to look at the world around me and let the beauty of it distract my mind that my breathing slowed to a normal rate and the desperation to surface subsided.

Not Our Natural Home

Though I learned to overcome the fear of breathing underwater, and later became certified as a recreational diver, it became very real to me that we are not meant to live in that world. It's not our natural habitat. The term SCUBA is an acronym for Self-Contained Underwater Breathing Apparatus—certainly something other than what came as original equipment at birth.

Several months after my initial diving experience, during my final SCUBA certification dive, I was reminded of this reality once again.

After the class settled at a depth of about forty-feet, we participated in a series of diving skills. What we were not aware of was that a secondary instructor was swimming up behind us turning off our oxygen. We became painfully aware of that fact when sucking on the regulator no longer produced the desired affect. We also became quickly aware that we either reached the surface or ceased to live. We had not forgotten the one rule of SCUBA: breathe. So, at forty-feet below the surface of the ocean with no oxygen, we, without hesitation, executed an emergency ascent.

As human beings living in this physical world we are designed to exist in an atmosphere rich with oxygen. Our bodies require it for life, and we thrive on it. From the moment we exit our mother's womb, it is unnatural—even impossible—for us to breathe liquid or to go without oxygen for more than a few minutes. When we stop breathing, we start dying. The number one rule of human life: breathe.

As spiritual beings living in a spiritual world, we are designed to exist in an atmosphere rich with Presence—God's presence. Our entire being requires it for life and thrives on it. From the day we are born again, it is unnatural for us to live without experiencing His life-giving, manifested presence. The songwriter put it this way,

> This is the air I breathe;
> This is the air I breathe;
> Your very presence living in me.
> And I, I'm desperate for You.
> And I, I'm lost without You.[1]

Paul made this clear when he stood before the crowd on Mars Hill and declared,

> *In Him we live and move and have our being*
> (Acts 17:28).

32

God's presence is our natural habitat, our authentic context for life. Any other context is foreign and deadly territory.

The Presence

Let me make a few things clear regarding the Presence. First, God's presence is not a mood, an atmosphere, or a feeling—though it influences our mood, transforms the atmosphere, and can certainly be felt. In fact, the Presence is not an "it" at all—but rather a person, specifically, the person of the Holy Spirit.

Second, let's be clear that living in the Presence is not an event, but a position—a living condition. It is living in an intimate relationship with God through His Spirit. Experiencing and enjoying the manifestation of His presence is our privilege, but it cannot be disconnected from our relationship with Him. To separate an experience in God from the person of God is to prostitute the Presence.

Third, living in His presence is the privilege of every believer. Jesus, when talking about the Holy Spirit who would come after He ascended to the Father, stated that every believer would receive the Spirit—a flowing river's worth.

> *He who believes in Me, as the Scripture has said, out of his heart will flow rivers of living water. But this He spoke concerning the Spirit, whom those believing in Him would receive...* (John 7:38, 39).

This is not the context for a privileged few but for all who believe.

When we choose to live in and from His presence, our

33

world is filled with all the delights of God. The psalmist David understood the beauty of this truth long before the cross.

> *In Your presence is fullness of joy; at Your right hand are pleasures forevermore* (Psalm 16:11).

Let me express David's thought this way: wherever God is, He is fully present. In other words, in God's presence, everything God is, is present with Him. Think about it this way: God's peace, mercy, favor, wisdom, knowledge, and power are present where He is. Where God is, all of His comfort, patience, love, joy, faithfulness and strength are in full play.

Now, think on this: when we live in His presence, all His pleasures, or delights, are where we are! They are all available to us. No wonder Paul wrote,

> *For in Him* [Jesus] *dwells all the fullness of the Godhead bodily, and you are complete in Him...* (Colossians 2:9-10).

His Presence: Hope's Home

So what does this have to do with our primary focus of hope? Everything. It is in the reality of God's presence that hope finds its authentication and substance. Outside of this context, hope is nothing more than wishful thinking that cannot be sustained when hopeless circumstances invade our world.

In the days following the sudden, unexpected death of our thirty-one-year-old daughter, Amy, mother of two young children, I found it difficult to sleep most nights.

Under the weight of grief, I would go downstairs and find a place on our living room couch, turn on the reading lamp, and begin to leaf through the Bible for something to comfort and console me.

Each night, to my surprise and disappointment, only a few minutes would pass before I would put the Bible down on the couch next to me and turn off the reading lamp. I had not found anything that helped give meaning to this senseless loss. With tears slowly rolling down my cheeks I would sit in the dark room filled with disquieting, troubling thoughts.

One night, the Presence settled into the room and surrounded me like a warm blanket. I could feel the Father sitting on the couch next to me, and we just sat there quietly together—no words exchanged between us. His comfort was tangible and settled deep into my spirit. It was in that atmosphere that hope began to come alive in me again, and I began the journey from being a prisoner of my circumstance to being a prisoner of hope.

It was in His manifest presence that I found one of God's most powerful and engaging delights—hope. I have discovered it to be abundant both in quantity and quality.

> *May the God of your hope so fill you with all joy and peace in believing [through the experience of your faith] that by the power of the Holy Spirit you may abound and be overflowing (bubbling over) with hope* (Romans 15:13, AMP).

Endnote

1. "Breathe," Marie Barnett. Copyright 1999, Vineyard Music.

When you say a situation
or a person is hopeless, you are
slamming the door in
the face of God.

—Charles L. Allen

CHAPTER THREE

I Choose Hope

I BELIEVE THE MOST POWERFUL tool we have in our personal tool belt is choice. We make hundreds, if not thousands, of choices every day from the time we wake up until we drift off to sleep at night. Every choice has consequences. Some may be insignificant while others can determine life changes, shorten or prolong our lives, or set monumental, even irreversible, events in motion.

Dr. Paul Chappell, pastor of Lancaster Baptist Church, wrote the following in his daily devotional of September 27, 2009:

> *God has given us the power of choice, but once we have made the choice, it has power over us.*

If this is true, and I suspect it usually is, then it would seem important that we pay attention to the choices we make. A single choice can have lasting influence.

The Impact of Choice

Adam and Eve made a choice in the Garden, and unfortunately, we continue to deal with the consequences to this day. Jesus chose to be obedient to the Father all the way to the cross, and thankfully, we reap the benefit of that choice now and for all of eternity. Joshua's declaration, "As for me and my house, we will serve the Lord,"[1] reflects a choice he made years before that set the course of his life while also challenging a nation to righteousness.

Today, choices will be made that will have impact on our world. They are powerful, and we have the choice to choose our choices.

As a child, I was susceptible to bronchial infections. Though my resistance to infection increased as an adult, it was not unusual for me to have a bout with bronchitis once a year. In the months following Amy's death this condition became chronic and dangerous. All the medicines and treatments that in the past had been effective in bringing relief no longer cleared the congestion or eased the labored breathing.

It was during a particularly intense episode that I came to a crisis moment and learned a lesson on the importance and power of choice.

Late one night, having been unable to sleep for several nights, I was fighting for air. Still held in the grief of my loss, I got out of bed. Gripped by the thought that this condition was now my future, troubling questions invaded my mind and assaulted my hope.

- Is this what happens to people who lose a daughter?

- Could it be that I am going to live the rest of my life emotionally crippled by grief and physically incapacitated?

- Is my contribution to my family and my community now at an end?

- Are my dreams now dead—laying at the feet of my circumstances?

Empowered to Choose

Death, in that moment, was not my fear; living in this debilitating condition was what scared me and was pushing me toward hopelessness. Then the Holy Spirit broke through my anxiety and reminded me of the passage regarding Abraham.

> *Who, contrary to hope, in hope believed, so that he became the father of many nations...* (Romans 4:18).

Though I have read the accounts of Abraham's life, and Paul's use of his story to illustrate faith many times, I had not noticed the extent of Abraham's dilemma regarding hope: "contrary to hope, in hope believed."

Abraham had every reason to not be hopeful about becoming a father, let alone the father of nations. Though he had the promise from God, he faced some overwhelming history and circumstances, both of which declared that the promise would never happen.

Think about this: Abraham and Sarah's history was not the kind of story that engendered hope. Sarah had been barren all of her life. There had never been a "window of opportunity" that would spark hope to where fertility would return to her body anytime soon. They had carried the promise for many years, and yet, Sarah continued to be unable to conceive. The attempt at making the promise come true by Abraham's producing a son through Sarah's servant, Hagar, proved to be less than a winning strategy.

Abraham's present circumstances, as recorded in Romans 4, were no more encouraging and could not be any more defeating or conclusive. He was a hundred years old, and his reproductive ability was now dead. Even if he had wanted to try again what he tried with Sarah's handmaiden, it was impossible. Added to this, his wife, Sarah, was about his same age, and her womb had not only consistently been unfruitful, the hope of fertility was now verifiably beyond reason. These are the facts—end of story.

Abraham faced two conflicting realities: the facts and the truth. The facts: Abraham's history and circumstances declared he would not be a father of nations. The truth: God had promised a son. It was between these two realities, or contexts, that Abraham had to choose. In choosing to live in the truth in the face of hopeless facts, Abraham chose hope—"contrary to hope, in hope believed."

As I sat on my couch that night contemplating my future and staring at that verse, I realized that hope was a choice I had the power to make. Though I was struggling to breathe and ached with grief, I realized I could choose between being a prisoner of my circumstances or a prisoner of hope. I had the power to choose between being held captive by situations I seemed to have no control over, or be captivated by liberating, life-giving, faith-producing hope.

From deep within my heart and out of my mouth, came this raspy, oxygen-starved shout, "I choose hope."

I Choose Hope

It is hard to describe what happened in that moment. It was as if I stepped out of a silent black-and-white horror movie into a surround-sound, high-definition, feel-good motion picture. My circumstances had not changed, but my context for life had. By choosing hope, I became open to new possibilities. It was then that God began to remind me of all the promises He has spoken over my life. Not only had hope been given fresh life, faith to realize those promises began to grow.

Belief Nurtured in Hope

We all are familiar with Abraham's great faith—it's the stuff legends are made of. Yet we may not have realized that his faith had a starting place—"in hope." It was while standing in hope that he believed.

>   ...In hope, believed...

Abraham's great faith was born out of hope. Hope is the parent of faith—the fertile ground in which the seed of faith is planted and grows. The writer of Hebrews makes this plain when he declares,

>   Now faith is the substance of things hoped for,
>   the evidence of things not seen (11:1).

Proverbs 13:12 is a much-quoted verse about hope.

>   Hope deferred makes the heart sick....

It is accurate to interpret Solomon's words as saying when what we hoped for is long in coming (deferred) the heart becomes sick in the waiting. Most likely, we have all experienced that delay between the promise and its fulfillment—the wait between the onset of hoping for something and the reality of that which is hoped for. *When will it ever come?* is often the cry of the heart becoming sick or discouraged.

In my journey to hope over the last several years, I have begun to see this verse in a different way, and I believe this view is just as accurate, especially in light of a New Testament passage. Here is my personal, amplified version of Proverbs 13:12:

> *When hope is abandoned, the heart becomes sick and vulnerable to disease.*

Allow me to explain. Paul, when writing about hope, makes the following statements:

> *For we were saved in this hope, but hope that is seen is not hope; for why does one still hope for what he sees? But if we hope for what we do not see, we eagerly wait for it with perseverance* (Romans 8:24, 25).

It seems to me Paul is inferring that the very nature of hope is made for the time of waiting—for that time when what we hope for has not yet arrived. The fact that we must wait for things to develop and come to pass is the very reason hope exists. If there is no waiting, there is no need for hope.

Therefore, it must be true that the heart does not become sick from simply waiting, but rather, in the midst of waiting, the heart becomes sick when hope is abandoned. Could it be that along with saying, "a hope unrealized makes the heart sick," Solomon is also saying, "hope abandoned makes the heart sick"?

I Choose Hope

Hope is my choice. It is always an available option. If I find it missing, it is because I have chosen to abandon it; hope has certainly not chosen to abandon me. We cannot always determine our circumstances, and our history is what it is. But we can choose to live in hope. In so doing, we reap the benefits of hope.

Forlorn Hopes

By way of introducing the following chapters, allow me to share a historical picture that has often challenged me in my journey.

I was reading a historical novel while on vacation when I came across the narrative of a military siege that took place on March 5, 1799, at the island city of Mysore by British troops attempting to deal with the troublesome Tipu Sultan. There were several interesting elements to the story, but the one that caught my attention was the description of the British troops known as the Forlorn Hopes. I was so intrigued by this band of soldiers that I researched them and found that they were not the imagination of the novelist but an actual, existing troop within the British army.

The very nature of hope is made for the time of waiting.

In an assault on a walled city, the most common tactic was to pound the base of the wall with cannon balls until it collapsed on itself creating an opening that could be scaled, giving the army immediate access to the city. This opening is referred to as "the breach." An advance troop would then assault the opening while the rest of the army waited for these troops to take the breach and secure the access into the city. These breach-takers were known as the Forlorn Hopes.

Securing the breach was the most dangerous part of the assault, and casualties among this elite group of men was extremely high. Yet, though the possibility of death was greater than the likelihood of survival, the Forlorn Hopes unit was comprised entirely of volunteers, both officers and men, who often competed for the honor of serving in this mission.

The reason these men would vie for the right to put their lives in such danger was that, along with the risk, there was the hope of great reward. Those among the Forlorn Hopes who survived the assault would receive the benefit of promotion and/or a cash reward. These men did not come from wealthy families or have influence in high places, so joining the Forlorn Hopes was their only road to advancement and profit. They were truly forlorn men, and the potential for gain with the promise of promotion made them desperate enough to charge the breach. They chose hope.

I would say they lived, and often died, in hopeful desperation.

Endnote

1. Joshua 24:15.

If it were not
for hope,
the heart would break.

—Thomas Fuller

CHAPTER FOUR

Hopeful

Desperation

O NE OF MY NEW FAVORITE QUOTES comes from that great theologian Dr. Seuss—you know, the famous poet-illustrator that wrote such spiritual works as *Green Eggs and Ham* and *How the Grinch Stole Christmas.* Anyway, I ran across his quote one day while looking up material on the subject of love and was captivated by how much it relates to hope as well.

> *You know you're in love when you don't want to go to sleep because your reality has become greater than your dreams.*

Wow! A reality greater than our dreams...! Is that

feasible? Is it biblical? It sounded more like a pipe dream than a possibility. Yet, as I thought on the picture Dr. Seuss' quote created in my mind, the Holy Spirit chose to jump in on my musings. He reminded me of Ephesians 3:20, a verse that has always attracted my attention and stirred my expectations.

> *Now to Him who is able to do exceedingly abundantly above all that we ask or think, according to the power that works in us.*

Paul made a declaration implying that we were fashioned to have realities greater than our dreams. This is made possible by the power that works in us. Could it be that we are to not just see this as a distant possibility but as something on which we should be setting our expectations—our hope?

Not convinced? Read that same verse from the Amplified Bible:

> *Now to Him Who, by (in consequence of) the* [action of His] *power that is at work within us, is able to* [carry out His purpose and] *do superabundantly, far over and above all that we* [dare] *ask or think* [infinitely beyond our highest prayers, desires, thoughts, hopes or dreams]— (AMP).

Greater Realities

Think about this: Abram dreamt of having a son, but he became Abraham, the father of nations. Joseph dreamt of authority over his father and brothers, but he was given influence and power over a nation, second only to Pharaoh. Hannah longed for a child—any child—but birthed a son that would be the prophetic voice for Israel. Naomi pined for an heir to continue her family lineage but God provided a grandson that would become the great-grandfather of King David and be counted in the ancestry of Jesus Christ.

There's more. The man who was lame from birth and who sat at the Gate Beautiful dreamt of someone placing a few coins in his alms bowl, but he ended up healed—leaping and running and praising God. The thief on the cross dreamt of being remembered by Jesus. He was not only remembered but he was also given a royal invitation into Paradise. Mary dreamt of a husband and a family, never imagining she would carry the Messiah in her womb and raise the Son of God.

These stories and many more illustrate reality greater than dreams, actuality superior to imagination.

Personal Dreaming

As a young boy, I was fascinated by the music and lifestyle of the gospel quartet. My parents, desiring to encourage my love for music, would take me to venues where three or four of these traveling singing groups would put on all-night concerts. The Stamps, The Oak Ridge Boys, The Blackwood Brothers, along with other lesser-known quartets and trios, would sing their well-practiced harmonies with enthusiasm and share their homespun stories of God's work in the lives of humanity. I would sit there mesmerized by the whole presentation.

After the concert, the groups would sometimes allow members of the audience to tour their huge, impressive traveling buses that were lined up and parked outside the concert hall. I don't know if I took advantage of that opportunity every time I attended a concert, but I remember at least one time stepping up into the luxury bus and feeling as if I was stepping into a dream.

I would leave those concerts with several albums under my arm and a dream in my heart. I don't believe it was so much a personal dream of mine to be a vocational gospel quartet singer—though I did actually travel as one for a year during my college days. It was more about the dream of traveling throughout the States in some kind of ministry that I held deep in my heart.

A few decades later, as I sat before the students in our supernatural school relating some of my ministry experiences, it dawned on me that I was actually living in a far greater reality than my dreams had ever revealed. Not only have I ministered numerous times across the United States, I have also been to over 30 nations, ministered in 23 of them, and am the founder and international director of supernatural schools in Fiji and the Philippines. Flying over 100,000 miles each year is normal life for me.

I would not even begin to credit my life adventure to my skills or my efforts. I am more surprised than anyone that I have been blessed in this way. I simply share this story to illustrate that I am living a greater reality than my dream as a young man—something far above and beyond what I could have ever asked or thought.

What About You?

Do you have room in your life for a greater reality? If you do, then I think it is appropriate to ask the question: How does this "above and beyond" become our reality? Or, how do we move from small dreams to greater realities? Paul makes it clear that this is made possible by the power that is at work within us.

Another appropriate question is "What...?," or more accurately, "Who is this power?" Again, Paul makes it plain that this power is the person of the Holy Spirit who makes His home inside of us.

> *Do you not know that your body is the temple of the Holy Spirit who lives within you* (1 Corinthians 6:19)?

I would suggest that our realities becoming greater than our dreams is made possible when we partner with the One who lives within us through what I call "hopeful desperation."

Desperation Defined

In its traditional usage, desperation is characterized by a reckless position or action brought on by despair, bordering on the edge of hopelessness. This is a desperation born out of fear, and it drives us to seek safety and security above significance and destiny. It is driven by the fear of loss rather than empowered by the hope of gain.

We hear this fearful, despair-driven desperation in the words of the ten men that returned from spying out the Promised Land.

> *We are not able to go up against the people, for they are stronger than we... the land through which we have gone as spies is a land that devours its inhabitants... there we saw the giants... and we were like grasshoppers in our own sight, and so we were in their sight... If only we had died in the land of Egypt! Or if*

only we had died in this wilderness! Why has the LORD brought us to this land to fall by the sword, that our wives and children should become victims?... Let us select a leader and return to Egypt (Numbers 13:31-33; 14:2-4).

Can you hear their desperation coming from the fear of loss? They lost sight of the potential, only seeing the obstacle. As a result, they became overwhelmed with despair, withdrawing from their destiny.

Our realities becoming greater than our dreams is made possible when we partner with the One who lives within us.

There is, however, a desperation born out of hope. It is this desperation that I am addressing here. This kind of desperation is birthed out of the expectation for a greater reality and is focused on the potential for significant gain. It empowers us to believe for, and activate, more than we can ask or think. It does not live in the realm of, "What if...?" but in the atmosphere of, "Why not?" Desperation in this context is best defined as being absolutely convinced of a potential.

This is the desperation of Caleb as he challenged the people to take the Land God had promised them. His words stand in stark contrast to those of his fellow spies. Here is the David Crone amplified version of Caleb's hopeful desperation:

People, this is our moment. This day is the culmination of the plan our God set into motion when he brought Joseph through betrayal and rejection and then gave him the power to save the fledgling nation of his father, Israel. This is why He protected us in Egypt, giving us a place to grow and become strong. It was for this moment that our God took Moses out of the wilderness and placed him before Pharaoh and used him to take us out of Egypt.

Everything we have hoped for as a people is on the other side of that river, and our God is waiting to partner with us for it to become our reality. That Land is our destiny, our inheritance. It will not be without its challenges or its risk. But the Land of our promise is an exceedingly good Land, and with our God, the people currently in that Land will be our lunch.

Are we desperate enough to risk it all in hope, to let go of our present reality in order to take hold of a greater one? I say, "Yes!" This is not the time to hesitate and miss the potential of this moment. It is the time to go into the Land and take hold of our destiny.

Breakthrough to Hopeful Desperation

Most of my life was lived under the shadow of the fear of failure. It colored every choice I made and often locked me out of divine opportunities. When I think of all the years of wasted potential, I am amazed that anything of eternal value was ever accomplished. I am convinced that any purposeful accomplishment in those years was possible only by the grace of God, and often, in spite of me. It just shows the amazing tenacity of God to accomplish His purposes on the earth.

There are several moments in my memory when living the way I described above began to shift. One of them stands out now as I write this chapter.

I was sitting in the morning session of Tommy Barnett's pastors' school in Phoenix, Arizona, when Tommy began to talk about a new ministry he was starting in Los Angeles called The Dream Center. I was impressed with the vision and knew the Lord was nudging me to give toward it.

Before I narrate that moment further, let me fill in some necessary background. For well over a year, the people of The Mission had been raising funds for a new sanctuary we were convinced was the will of God. Progress was very slow. As a leadership we had determined that we would only build with cash and were committed to not borrow any funds. As a part of this commitment, we agreed that we would not begin the project until we had one million dollars in the bank. At the time I attended the pastors' school, we had only $120,000 of the necessary total in the church savings account. It was evident in the natural that at the present rate, it would be many years before anything could be done to begin building.

It was in this context that I walked up the hill overlooking the church in Phoenix and heard the Holy Spirit say, "Give it all." There was no doubt in my mind what the Holy Spirit was asking. I also was aware that He was offering a partnership. It was as if I could hear the heart of Caleb in my spirit: *Are you desperate enough to risk it all in hope, to let go of your present reality in order to take hold of a greater one? This is not the time to hesitate and miss the potential of the moment.*

54

My response to the invitation of the Holy Spirit on that day would move me from fearful desperation to hopeful desperation and transform the way I would live my life from that moment on. Thanks to the courage given to all of us at The Mission by the Holy Spirit, we gave our entire building fund to The Dream Center. On April 23rd of that year, we handed the check to Tommy Barnett as he stood on the platform in the gymnasium we were using as our sanctuary.

Following that day, however, we had no idea how we would ever complete, let alone begin, the construction of the sanctuary. But we were learning to live in hopeful desperation. Exactly one year from the day we gave Tommy his check, we had one million dollars in our bank account. Some of the story of how the Holy Spirit partnered with us to bring this miracle about is found in my book, *The Power of Your Life Message.*[1] But let me say here that our reality did become greater than our dreams, and we witnessed many more miraculous provisions totaling $3,800,000 and completed a 37,000-square-foot sanctuary debt-free.

I live with this challenge always in my heart:

- How absolutely convinced am I of the potential for a greater reality?

- Am I living today in the desperation born of fear or of hope?

Every day presents this option, and every day I must choose.

Endnote

1. Crone, David. *The Power of Your Life Message.* Available at: store.iMissionChurch.com.

A leader is a dealer in hope.

—Napoleon Bonaparte

CHAPTER FIVE

Testing Your

Desperation

WHILE THINKING ONE DAY on hopeful desperation, I began to write a list of things that would help me measure the quality of my hopeful desperation. This list has become my "You know you're living in hopeful desperation when—"-test.

You know you're living in hopeful desperation when— the price cannot stop you.

It is no secret that I love food—good food. In fact, I even enjoy talking about it. One of the delightful experiences of eating in a fine restaurant for me is reading the menu out loud as if I were reciting well-written poetry. I even enjoy listening to the waiter or waitress describe the chef's special preparation. It is truly a spiritual experience.

On one of our recent trips to Maui, Deborah and I dined at the Lahaina Grill in downtown Lahaina, known for its fine cuisine and especially famous for its Triple Berry Pie. With the danger of hyperbole in mind, allow me to relate the experience to you.

After reading through the menu and finding nothing that seemed to satisfy my palette, I hungrily awaited the waitress' description of that night's specials. As she began to lyrically depict the luscious preparation of a 14-ounce rib-eye steak, the heavens opened up, and I was caught up into culinary realms of glory. Before she could finish and prior to her quoting the price, I responded in hopeful desperation, "I'll take it."

It is with great joy that I tell you the meal lived up to its billing. It was an epicurean delight—absolute Heaven on Earth—and the price held no consequence. When the exorbitant bill arrived at the table, my only exclamation was, "It was worth every penny!" Oh, by the way, the Triple Berry Pie was also delicious, as usual.

Living in hopeful desperation allows us to see past the cost and focus on the potential gain. We make choices considering the possibilities of increase rather than the expense of the attempt. This is not ignoring the price, but refusing to allow the price to determine our decisions.

Planning is good. Letting the fear of loss determine our choices—not good.

Shadrach, Meshach, and Abednego were three young Hebrew men living in captivity under the rule of the ruthless King Nebuchadnezzar. These three contemporaries of Daniel came face-to-face with the choice between fearful or hopeful desperation when refusal to worship the golden statue of the king meant death in a fiery furnace. To obey the demand of the king and bow to the statue would compromise their faith; yet to refuse to bow would lead to their demise. This was a desperate situation.

Their response to the king's demand was to live in hopeful desperation, and their actions declared that the price would not keep them from serving and worshiping the one, true God.

> *O Nebuchadnezzar, we have no need to answer you in this matter... Our God whom we serve is able to deliver us from the burning fiery furnace, and He will deliver us from your hand, O king. But if not, let it be known to you, O king, that we do not serve your gods, nor will we worship the gold image which you have set up* (Daniel 3:16-18).

Right now, as I write this chapter, there are hundreds of thousands of Christians in Iraq faced with this very same desperate circumstance. A radical Islamic sect invaded and took control of some of the oldest Christian settlements on Earth. They demanded that the Christians convert to Islam or face the loss of everything, up to and including their very lives. This is not ancient Bible history but a current reality. These believers are right now choosing their desperation—one born out of fear or one born out of hope.

You and I may not be facing life-threatening choices like the friends of Daniel or the Christians in Iraq, but we are often confronted with the cost of pursuing a greater reality. We risk the loss of relationships with those who do not understand and believe us to be too radical. There is always the potential of apparent failure when we step out in faith. The loss of our reputation is not out of the realm of possibility.

The price tag for not settling for mediocrity can be high. The question is, are we desperate enough to live in hope and not let the cost of our pursuit stop us?

You know you're living in hopeful desperation when— shame cannot stop you.

Picture this: One of the top religious leaders of the city is hosting the most popular spiritual personality and miracle worker of the day. Many important people have been invited to observe the event as the two leaders sit down to have a meal and converse on various topics. Without a doubt the air was electric with anticipation.

Then, the unthinkable happens. In walks an uninvited guest, a woman. And not just any woman, a prostitute! Not only does she come into the courtyard where the Pharisee and Jesus are reclining while eating, she kneels behind Jesus and begins to wail loudly, washing His feet with her tears and wiping them with her long hair. She then does the unspeakable: she kisses His feet unashamedly and will not stop.

This behavior would be shameful in most settings, but can you imagine how thick the shame-on-you atmosphere was in the courtyard that day? We know some of what the Pharisee was thinking because Jesus exposed it, and the disciple Luke was there to record it.

> *This man, if he were a prophet, would know who and what manner of woman this is who is touching Him, for she is a sinner* (Luke 7:39).

The Pharisee's disdain was aimed at both Jesus and the woman.

But this woman had seen her window of opportunity and acted in hopeful desperation as if she were declaring,

Testing Your Desperation

"This is my moment for a greater reality." She refused to allow the shame of her own sinful past, nor the shame being heaped on her from nearly everyone there, stop her from getting what she came for.

Jesus did not disappoint this desperate woman, for He released what she needed: forgiveness, love, and peace. This woman came into that courtyard living in a nightmare and left in a reality greater than her dreams.

All of us have history that we would rather forget. There are events, conversations, actions, outbursts, and failures that cause us to cringe when we recall them. The shame of those times can be formidable barricades to our breakthroughs and advancement. That is, unless we choose to live in hopeful desperation.

One of my first international trips was to the nation of Ivory Coast, West Africa. The missionary stationed there was my good friend, Fauzi. We had attended Bible school together, and I was excited to be on the field with him. This trip was also one of the first times I preached using an interpreter. That experience, however, was not a pleasant one.

The meeting was located in a classroom where 30 or 40 people had gathered to receive ministry. I was aware that many of those in the room had walked for several miles to attend the session and would walk the same miles back home after the meeting. They were hungry people having paid a price to be there. You could feel the anticipation building in the room, and I was beginning to feel the weight of the responsibility of ministering to these precious people. I was also feeling the pressure of not wanting to disappoint neither them nor my friend.

When it came time for me to speak, I realized that I was not prepared for what was about to happen. It became evident from the first sentence of my greeting that I was a novice being thrown into a situation only the most experienced speaker could cope with. As I spoke the first sentence, Fauzi interpreted it into the national language of French. This would have been manageable except that he then interpreted his French into one of the local dialects.

If you have ever experienced speaking through an interpreter, you know how important rhythm and flow are in helping you keep your train of thought. One interpretation takes practice, having two interpretations has a tendency to throw off even an experienced speaker. But what happened next made it impossible for me to even remember what I had said, let alone think of what I wanted to say next.

Planning is good. Letting the fear of loss determine our choices—not good.

After Fauzi interpreted into French then into a local dialect, another man interpreted into yet two other dialects. It was now four interpretations later, and it was again my turn to speak. I was speechless. I stared in agonizing silence at the people gathered in front of me. They looked back at me with eager expressions, expecting to hear something of eternal value coming from my mouth. It was quickly apparent that was not going to happen.

With sweat now running down my face, I finally struggled to speak another sentence and then waited for what seemed like several minutes for the interpretations to be completed. During the delay, I tried unsuccessfully to put my thoughts together. When it was once again my turn, I stood in stunned silence while those hungry people stared back with anticipation. Things did not improve.

Testing Your Desperation

The long delay continued to so disquiet me that I could not connect any coherent thoughts. Out of desperation, I opted to end the message, prayed over them, and quickly left the room feeling devastated.

I was deeply disappointed that I had let my friend down, but most of all, I was ashamed that I had wasted the time of those amazing, hungry people. I responded to that experience in fearful desperation and declared, "I will never speak through an interpreter again!" And for many years, I kept that promise. My shame kept me from living in the greater reality God planned for me.

Then, Jehovah-sneaky created in me such a love for the nations that I agreed to an invitation to speak at the national convention of the Assemblies of God in the nation of Fiji. I accepted the assignment before I realized I would have to speak through an interpreter. It was time to choose: run in fearful desperation or respond in hopeful desperation and declare, "This is my moment, my chance for a greater reality." I chose the latter, choosing to join with the Forlorn Hopes.

That trip opened up a whole new world to me.

You know you are living in hopeful desperation when— the crowd cannot stop you.

The crowd is the place of everyone's opinion but with little or no revelation. It is where tradition trumps advancement and efficiency is more important than effectiveness. The crowd exerts a tremendous amount of influence aimed at keeping the status quo, preserving image, and protecting sameness. It has a vested interest in holding you and your present reality within its borders.

A man that had known nothing but darkness all his life took up his usual place on the side of the road and waited for someone to drop a few coins in his lap. His name was

63

Bartimaeus, and this was his position—his reality—in life.

As Bartimaeus settled in for the day and waited for his provision, a large multitude of people began passing by his station and pressed in close to where he was seated. Curious as to what all the commotion was about, the blind man asked those nearest him, "What's going on?"

He could sense the crowds were intently focused on something important, so he inquired again, this time with a louder voice.

"What's happening here?" Anticipation and excitement in the air was unmistakable.

"Jesus of Nazareth is passing by," they answered him. Bartimaeus had heard stories of this Jesus healing lepers, the lame, and those like him—the blind. He was immediately interested and wondered if this could be his moment—his chance for a greater reality. He was desperate, but dare he hope?

He knew he had to take advantage of his opportunity, so he cried out in a loud voice,

> *Jesus, Son of David, have mercy on me!* (Luke 18:38)

The crowd was not pleased with Bartimaeus' outburst. They tried to silence him, embarrassed by his forward behavior. What right did he have to act outside the crowd?

The choice of a lifetime now faced blind Bartimaeus—fear the crowd and remain silent or act in hopeful desperation and reach in faith for a greater reality. He chose to ignore the crowd and yelled all the louder.

Testing Your Desperation

Son of David, have mercy on me! (v. 39)

Jesus responded to Bartimaeus' desperation with a question:

What do you want Me to do for you...? (v. 41)

Bartimaeus did not hesitate to make his request known:

Lord, I want to see! (NIV)

The next words of Jesus would radically transform his reality.

Arise, go your way. Your faith has made you well (v. 42).

In other words, "Get on with life. This place where you are living is no longer your identity."

The crowds are all around us. They are not evil; they are just stuck in their lifeless traditions, living in a fearful desperation to keep things just as they are. When we live in hopeful desperation, however, we refuse to be immobilized by the influence of the crowds and are free to pursue a greater reality.

You know you are living in hopeful desperation when— rejection cannot stop you.

We never think of Jesus as being someone who would reject or purposefully offend someone coming to Him with a desperate need. Yet we find this very thing in Matthew's and Mark's gospels as they relate the story of a Greek Gentile mother whose daughter needed His help.

65

The woman came to Jesus the first time with a desperate cry.

> *Lord, Son of David, have mercy on me! My daughter is demon-possessed and suffering terribly* (Matthew 15:22, NIV).

Jesus ignored her, refusing to even talk to her. It is obvious from the narrative that this did not stop her as she continued to follow Jesus and His disciples declaring aloud her need. The woman's incessant crying so aggravated the disciples that they urged Jesus to send her away. Jesus, it appears, affirms their request in His response.

> *I was sent only to the lost sheep of Israel* (v. 24).

Even this second rejection does not keep the woman from pursuing a greater reality for her daughter who desperately needed deliverance. Instead of withdrawing, she throws herself at the feet of Jesus and presents her case again. Jesus' answer is rather startling.

> *It is not good to take the children's bread and throw it to the little dogs* (v. 26, NKJV).

Jesus not only rejected this hurting, desperate woman, but He offended her, referring to her and her daughter as "dogs" not worthy of His attention. This kind of rejection and offense would crush most people and have them angrily walking away, eliminating any chance of help by heatedly attacking the source. But not this woman. She was hopefully desperate and responded to Jesus with tenacity and faith.

Testing Your Desperation

Yes, Lord, yet even the little dogs eat the crumbs which fall from their master's table (v. 27).

This desperate mother seized the moment in hope and Jesus' response to her faith set her daughter free.

Woman, you have great faith! Your request is granted (v. 28 NIV).

I think it is accurate to say that most of us are way too easily offended, especially by rejection. I hate to think of all the times that I have failed to press through with a potential breakthrough just because of the fear of rejection. Living in fear of the pain of rejection will always be an insurmountable obstacle to a greater reality. But when we choose to live in hopeful desperation, the obstruction of rejection cannot stop us, and it becomes the stepping-stone into fresh, new territory.

You know you are living in hopeful desperation when— the forces of hell cannot stop you.

At times, most of us believe we have problems that are insurmountable, yet they pale in comparison to the problems of the man Jesus ran into after landing on the shore of the Gadarenes. We don't know his real name, but you may recognize the name he gave to Jesus, "Legion," a name descriptive of his condition. This man was so demon possessed that the people of the town tried to restrain him with chains and shackles, but he would simply break loose.

When Jesus showed up, Legion was living among the tombs, naked and in absolute torment. This was his reality. At that moment, every demon within him was screaming for him to stay away from Jesus. They had this man right where they wanted him, and they did not want to let go. But Legion was desperate for a greater reality.

Mark's Gospel records what happened.

> *When He saw Jesus from afar, he ran and worshiped Him* (5:6).

Hold on right here for a moment. Did you hear what you just read? A demon possessed man, opposed by the hellish reality in him, overcame that opposition and worshiped Jesus! A legion of anti-worshiping demons screaming inside this man's head, "Don't do it!" could not restrain his hopeful desperation.

In the last scene of this powerful story, we find this once-tormented and seemingly helpless man now sitting beside Jesus, fully clothed and in his right mind. In hopeful desperation, Legion stepped out of his nightmare into his greater reality.

This story has often challenged me when circumstances tempt me to back away from the potential gains God places in front of me. If Legion can choose to move in hopeful desperation while being opposed by demonic resident guests, what about me? No matter what the world—or hell itself—throws at me, I have living in me the One who empowers me to experience the exceedingly, abundantly above what I could ask or even think to ask.

Hopeful Desperation

It may be that we are facing costly choices or have been made to feel shamed by our pursuit of God and His call on our lives. We may be hearing the cries of those who wish to silence our voice of hope, and it feels as though demonic forces have conspired against us. This is not the time for us to cower in fear or respond in hopelessness. This is our day to stand up on the inside and choose to live in hopeful desperation.

The strongest principle of growth
lies in human choice.

—George Elliot

CHAPTER SIX

Why I Choose Hope

FRIEDRICH NIETZSCHE, A 19TH century German philosopher, held a rather cynical perspective on hope. He is probably most known for his statement, "God is dead," as well as his interest in Nihilism, the belief that nothing has any inherent importance and that life lacks purpose. In referencing hope, Nietzsche states:

> *Hope, in reality, is the worst of all evils because it prolongs the torments of man.*

This contemptuous view of hope reminds me of a quote I heard as a young man that I found humorous at the time:

> *I feel so much better now that I have given up hope.*[1]

PRISONER OF HOPE

I am not aware of the context in which it was stated by author Ashleigh Brilliant. However, as it stands, I no longer find the quote humorous and have come to reject it to the same degree that I reject Nietzsche's perspective.

Hope is not the worst of all evils, nor is it helpful for it to be abandoned. The truth is, without hope, there is none. Hal Lindsey, Christian author and speaker states:

> *Man can live about forty days without food, about three days without water, about eight minutes without air, but only for one second without hope.*

Hope is not an option for life.

Hope is found in the very nature of God and is, therefore, inherently good and of immense value. Paul makes it clear that it is one of three qualities that have endured the tests of time, circumstances, and the cynic.

> *And now abide* [endure, not depart, continue] *faith, hope, love, these three...* (1 Corinthians 13:13, author's comments).

Cleddie Keith, a pastor friend of mine states:

> *A man with an experience is never at the mercy of a man with an argument.*

I choose hope without apology and can honestly state that my experience in hope has left me without a competitive foe. Hope has been such a powerful giver of life that no argument can persuade me to abandon it. To misquote Forest Gump, "I'm not a smart man, but I know what hope is."

Why I Choose Hope

In the months following the death of our daughter, I began to make a list of the reasons why I choose hope. That list, along with some insights from my journey into supernatural, supercharged-hope, comprise much of the content of this chapter and those following. It continues to be a reminder of the importance of the choice I make intentionally every day.

Yes, each and every day I choose hope.

Though I have no interest in arguing with Nietzsche or Ashleigh Brilliant, I do desire to follow the Apostle Peter's encouragement:

> *Always be ready to give a defense to everyone who asks you a reason for the hope that is in you* (1 Peter 3:18).

Therefore, allow me to give you my reasons for choosing and living in hope.

I choose hope because hope is superior to hopelessness.

I cannot say that I have ever had a day of utter hopelessness. But I have come close enough to that cliff to know, without a doubt, it does not compare in any favorable way to the reality of hope.

In 2014, we had the privilege of hosting in our home several of the directors from Sounds of the Nations, one of whom was Josh Klinkenberg of New Zealand. Toward the end of his time with us, the three of us—Deborah, Josh, and myself—were sitting in our living room sharing some of our life experiences together. At some point during the conversation I made a passing reference to the death of our daughter Amy, not realizing Josh was unaware of that part of our recent history. Startled, Josh stopped me and asked, "You had a daughter who died? When did that happen?"

I briefly related the story and the time frame, after which Josh responded with amazement, "I have been with you in your home these past few days, and I never would have imagined you experienced such a tragic loss. You both are so healthy and full of life." That moment will live with us for the rest of our journey, and those words have become some of our most cherished encouragements. They also illustrate the wonder of the grace of God and underscore the power of hope over hopelessness.

Hope is the language of the Holy Spirit and the kingdom of God. It inspires within us the fruit of joy, faith, peace, life, and health. It is this God-anchored hope that keeps our hearts healthy, even in the most heart-wrenching losses of life.

We do not have to buy into hopelessness or give up hope, even in situations we know will never change. Indeed, these circumstances do exist. I cannot change the fact that my daughter no longer resides on this earth. I know she will not walk into the room and fill it with her laughter and personality, nor will I get to wrap my arms around her and comfort her, nor she me, in this lifetime.

However, I do not have to give up hope; instead I aim my hope at that which is eternal. I will see Amy again, and the hope of that reunion fills me with joy every day.

When we choose hopelessness, we are speaking the language of the kingdom of darkness, and hell comes only too readily into agreement with our negative position. Hopelessness produces the fruit of fear, despair, anxiety, depression, sickness, and death.

Hopelessness leaves us vulnerable to the diseases of the heart.

- **A hard heart**—one that has given up and become jaded because of disappointment or disillusionment.

- **A wounded or broken heart**—one that has become damaged through rejection or loss.

- **An impure heart**—one that has been exposed to infection through compromise driven by fear.

- **A diseased heart**—physical heart diseases brought on in part by the fruit of hopelessness as mentioned above.

Hope is superior in every way. In Scripture there are six adjectives that describe hope. One of them is an "unhealthy hope" referred to in Psalm 33:17 as "vain hope." Vain hope is empty of any substance, having been placed in something that is ultimately ineffective and limited. The other five adjectives we will explore, however, give us a great picture of the excellent and multifaceted nature of hope.

Good Hope

Paul refers to "good hope" in his second letter to the Thessalonians.

> *Now may our Lord Jesus Christ Himself, and our God and Father, who has loved us and given us everlasting consolation and **good hope** by grace, comfort your hearts and establish you in every good word and work* (2:16-17, emphasis added).

The word "good" means to be beneficial in its effect. In other words, hope produces a good result.

Blessed Hope

Paul refers to "blessed hope" in his letter to Titus when encouraging him in the things to come.

> Looking for the **blessed hope** and glorious appearing of our great God and Savior Jesus Christ (2:13, emphasis added).

"Blessed" is a word that is a true expression of one who is happy or supremely blessed. So, hope produces an atmosphere of blessed happiness.

Better Hope

The writer of the book of Hebrews writes of a "better hope" when comparing the inferior hope given by the Law to the superior hope of the New Covenant.

> On the other hand, there is the bringing in of a **better hope**, through which we draw near to God (7:19, emphasis added).

The word "better" speaks of that which is superior, advantageous, more useful, and more excellent in quality. This simply means that better hope is better!

Living Hope

Peter, when writing his first epistle, speaks of "living hope" as our place of residence.

> Blessed be the God and Father of our Lord

Why I Choose Hope

Jesus Christ, who...has begotten [birthed] *us again into a **living hope**...* (1:3, emphasis added).

The adjective "living" expresses the meaning of "that which is active and full of life." Hope, then, is an invigorating, life-producing quality.

Abundant Hope

In his letter to the Romans, Paul refers to an "abundant hope" as he prays for the believers in that city.

*Now may the God of hope fill you with all joy and peace in believing, that you may **abound in hope** by the power of the Holy Spirit* (15:13, emphasis added).

The word "abound" is one of my favorite words in Scripture. It means, "to overflow in quality and quantity." When we abound in hope, we are tapping into that which has an unlimited supply and superior quality.

What does all that reveal? Hope that is anchored in the God of all hope is superior to any other hope. This superior hope—

- is beneficial in producing good in and for us,

- surrounds us with an atmosphere of happiness and life, and

- overflows with quality and quantity.

With this understanding, we see that hope is superior in every way to hopelessness.

**I choose hope because hope sets
my focus on life.**

When we choose hope, our whole being is aimed at abundance, promise, and destiny. Choosing hope keeps us from being trapped in the circumstantial rationale for despair.

No Hanging Harps

One day I was mulling over the blessings I lost when Amy died. She was my biggest fan, and she always knew what to say to encourage me and brag on me. Her laugh was the most contagious sound in the world and always brought me great joy. Among other things, I began to think about the things she was missing and the joy she would have had in seeing her children grow.

Hope has been such a powerful giver of life that no argument can persuade me to abandon it.

It was only after a few minutes of this musing that I realized thinking about these things from a place of loss rather than a place of hope was not healthy for me. I was doing what the nation of Israel did when they were taken into Babylonian captivity: they sat by the river and remembered what they had lost. Psalms 137 records that they wept, refused to sing, and hung their harps on the willow trees.

I didn't want to go down that road, so I started a conversation with Holy Spirit about the things I have gained. I know this sounds a little strange, but it seemed hopeful to me to find a practical reason to be thankful in my time of pain. Martha Beck, renowned author and life coach states:

> *Hopeful thinking can get you out of your fear zone and into your appreciation zone.*

In this place of hope I heard Holy Spirit say, "You will never have to be anxious or worried about Amy ever again." If you are a father with a daughter, you know how liberating this revelation was to me. I love my boys and would do anything to protect them, but there was something different about my concern for my daughter Amy. There was not a day that she was alive on this earth that I was not thinking of her welfare and protection. But now I have the hope of her absolute safety and security.

The Reticular Activator

There is a part of our brain that regulates the things we focus on and take note of. Every day we are bombarded with visual and audio stimulation, and if our brain tried to take it all in and point it out to us, we would be driven absolutely crazy. The reticular activator is the part of our brain that keeps that from happening by determining what we focus on and what we ignore.

The reticular activator is calibrated by many of our choices. When you choose to buy a yellow car because you haven't seen many yellow cars, you can be sure that from that day on you will see almost nothing but yellow cars. You have calibrated your reticular activator to look for yellow cars and ignore the other colors.

Solomon may not have known about this part of his brain, but he surely understood the revelation when he wrote the following:

> *Trust in the Lord with all your heart and lean not on your own understanding. In all your ways acknowledge him and he will direct your path* (Proverbs 3:3-4).

He understood that whatever you acknowledge—recognize, give permission to, focus on—will set your direction.

Choosing to live in hope sets my reticular activator on life and truth. I then can see the roadway that leads to abundance and greater realities. A dear friend, Ivan Tait, says:

> *You will see what you look for, and you will find what you seek.*

If I fail to choose hope, my whole being will find reason to despair and give up. When I choose hope, I give my heart and mind the command, as well as the permission, to search out hopeful things. My focus will be on every part of life that engenders and encourages hope. In hope I see what God has done and is doing instead of focusing on what the enemy is doing or what my circumstances are declaring.

Norman Cousins, a famous promoter of holistic medicine states:

> *The human body experiences a powerful gravitational pull in the direction of hope. That is why the patient's hopes are the physician's secret weapon. They are the hidden ingredients in any prescription.*

I choose hope because I want my focus to be on the "above and beyond" that is my inheritance.

Endnote

1. Brilliant, Ashleigh Ellwood. *I Feel Much Better, Now That I've Given Up Hope: And Even More Brilliant Thoughts,* copyright 1984, Brilliant Enterprises.

I don't know what can be
so dangerous about giving
people hope.

—Joel Osteen

CHAPTER SEVEN

Hope's

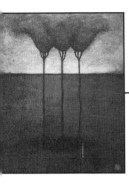

Influence

W E DO NOT LIVE IN A VACUUM as if separated from the atmosphere, circumstances, or people around us. This is also true of the choices we make. Our choices are not singular in their impact. When I choose hope, there is both targeted and co-lateral influence.

I choose hope because hope defies my negative circumstances.

Hope stands in the face of everything negative and declares, "You will not defeat me." It prophesies into overwhelming circumstances, "This will not be the day of my defeat."

Consider the journey of Joseph and you come to the conclusion that he was, without a doubt, a prisoner of hope. Nearly every part of his journey from the pit to the palace was filled with negative circumstances: rejection by his brothers, forced slavery, betrayal by Potipher's wife, imprisonment—all declaring the hopelessness of his situation.

Yet, Joseph excelled in spite of every trial and negative circumstance. How? I would suggest that he chose to continue to hope. Hope kept the door open to his destiny while closing the door to the declarations of his circumstances. At the dawning of each new day that Joseph found himself still under persecution, I can imagine he stood tall in his inner man and in hope declared, "You will not defeat me on this day!"

Though his brothers sold him into slavery, choosing hope empowered Joseph to view their actions not as opposing circumstances but as purposeful strategies of God.

And God sent me before you to preserve a posterity for you in the earth, and to save your lives by a great deliverance. So now it was not you who sent me here, but God... But as for you, you meant evil against me; but God meant it for good, in order to bring it about as it is this day, to save many people alive (Genesis 45:7-8; 50:20).

I will never forget the moment when Deborah and I walked out of the hospital emergency room leaving behind the body of our daughter. There has never been a more devastating moment in our lives than that one. Yet, as we walked across the parking lot to our car, a quiet yet determined pronouncement came from deep inside of Deborah, "I will not live mad, and I will not live sad." That declaration has become one of the main building blocks of our life's foundation that we continue to build on to this day. Deborah was choosing hope in the face of overwhelming loss, and it defied our pain, our hurt, and the prediction of our tragic circumstance.

Hope sees the invisible, feels the intangible, and achieves the impossible. When circumstance predicts my failure, hope promises my victory. When situations prophesy my doom, hope declares my advancement. When conditions project reversal, hope forecasts blessing. It may be that difficult events knock me down, but hope puts me back on my feet.

I choose hope because my hope is significant for everyone around me.

As believers, we should be the most hopeful people on the planet. We are living testaments of hope, and as such, we have an obligation—a privilege—to be influences for hope to everyone around us.

Our hope is not just about us. When we choose hope, we inspire others to do the same. Many years ago, I attended a pastors' school, led by Dr. Robert Schuller, the founding pastor of the Garden Grove Community Church in Garden Grove, California. During the school, he shared the story of building the Crystal Cathedral, a sanctuary whose walls and ceiling were constructed out of glass.

As he shared the story of the difficulty and expense of engineering and building an all-glass structure, he said something that has stuck with me to this day. He spoke of the opposition he faced in bringing his vision into reality. The engineering was considered nearly impossible, and the cost estimates seemed to escalate daily. On top of these difficulties, his critics were accusing him of trying to build a memorial to himself.

There came a time when the pressure was so great, he was tempted to heed the advice of some of his closest friends, as well as the judgment of his critics, and give up on his dream. As he contemplated that decision, he began to think about the impact of shutting down the project. "If I lose hope and give up on this vision, what will it mean to the pastor of the church in the little town in Michigan or the community in Texas that has been watching this journey? What will it do to their hope of building their dream? If I give up, will they give up too?"

Dr. Schuller did not give up, however, and he went on to solve the issues and built what many told him was impossible. He understood that as a man of hope and faith, he had the responsibility to influence and inspire others. The Crystal Cathedral stands today as an encouragement to those whose dreams stand in the balance. It is a testimony of the power of hope.

Living in hope is not just about us.

The following story is a very personal one. It is recounted in detail in my book, *The Power of Your Life Message,* but I believe it important to share an abbreviated version in this chapter.

At some point during the hours following the death of our daughter, I began to contemplate the possibility of resurrection. Jesus instructed us to heal the sick, raise the dead, and cast out demons. I had experienced two of the three but have not raised the dead. I had heard many stories of this happening but had not witnessed it. The more I thought about the potential of raising someone from the dead, the more a resolve formed in my heart and a fresh hope crept into my spirit. Could it be possible to raise my daughter from the dead? Though I had never done it, this seemed to be a good time to start.

I picked up the phone and called Graham Cooke, a friend and resident prophet in The Mission at that time. When he answered the phone, I heard myself say, "Graham, we want you and the church to stand with us and pray for Amy's resurrection."

He did not sound shocked but asked me a question, which, at the moment, I did not know how to answer. "What do you want us to do?"

"I don't know," I answered. I realized that I had just thrown down the gauntlet and there was no turning back. The next day was Father's Day Sunday, and we knew we would not be able to attend, so I responded, "Just let the congregation know that we are praying for Amy to be resurrected, and we invite them to join us." Graham agreed with enthusiasm, and we ended the conversation.

The next morning, the church community took on the challenge, and with great faith and enthusiasm, they prayed for death to be overturned. By Sunday afternoon the word had gone out literally around the world. Bill Johnson and Kris Vallotton from Bethel Church in Redding, California, were the first to call and join their churches with ours in the battle for resurrection. Then the troops from various places in the world began to report in, and the army continued to grow. Churches and friends from all over the United States, Australia, China, Hungary, Denmark, Fiji, Philippines, India, and England joined their prayers with ours in agreement to do what Jesus told us to do, " raise the dead."

Unchartered Territory

Over the next few days, we faced several challenges, not the least of which was the ability to physically lay hands on Amy's body. We were not experienced in raising the dead, but it seemed important that we be able to touch her while we prayed. However, the coroner's office was holding her body in preparation for a required autopsy and would not allow me to see or touch her.

On the evening before the autopsy was scheduled, I was able to reach an officer who was willing to help me at least get into the same building in which Amy's body was being held. I asked Dan McCollam, friend and colleague, to accompany me.

When we arrived at the morgue, a young man met us at the door and ushered us into the waiting area. He told me that it was not possible for me to go to the room where Amy's body was laid but that I could go into the adjacent room. The autopsy would take place later that day. I left Dano in the waiting area and entered the assigned room. I laid my hands on the wall I believed to be the adjoining wall to Amy's room and began to command life.

After about twenty minutes the young man returned and apologized, stating that he needed me to leave. As I started out the door, I asked him one more favor, "Officer, will you please go to my daughter's body and check her vitals?"

He looked at me with compassion and said, "Sir, she has no vital signs to check."

My response surprised even me, "I know she didn't before I prayed, but will you humor this father who has just lost his only daughter and please check?"

"Yes, of course," he replied. I went into the adjoining room and waited in hope with Dano.

I will never forget the look of compassion on the face of the officer as he came back into the room where we were waiting. With tears filling his eyes he said to me, "I'm sorry, there is no change." I thanked him for his kindness, and we left the building.

Still holding on to hope, I decided then and there we must try to lay hands on Amy one more time and pray for her resurrection! As a pastor, I have been around death often enough to know what an autopsy does to a person's body. In spite of the fact that the autopsy would have already taken place, I made plans with the mortuary director, Bridget, to come the next day and pray.

My father, two of my colleagues from The Mission, Dan McCollam and Bob Book, myself, and Ivan Tait, a dear friend who had come to be with us during this time, all met at the mortuary the next morning. We made our way to the room where Amy's body lay. Many others from The Mission had also

Hope sees the invisible, feels the intangible, and achieves the impossible.

gathered to stand with us in prayer. We did everything we knew to do. Bill Johnson had told me that in Mozambique they have seen hundreds of resurrections. They learned to pray over the feet first. If within fifteen minutes the feet begin to get warm, they know they will have a resurrection and so they continue to pray. If this does not happen, the person will most likely not be resurrected no matter how long they pray.

Gathered around Amy's body, we took this strategy to heart and began to pray over her feet. Our team commanded Amy to live, declaring life over her body. After nearly thirty minutes of praying, however, we knew Amy was not coming back. At this point, I asked everyone to leave the room. I sat in a chair next to Amy's body, and with my hand on her arm, I had my last fatherly chat with my daughter.

Viral Hope

We did not get the resurrection that we were hoping for that day. However, I have come to realize that pressing through with faith into unchartered territory may not achieve immediate results. The important thing to remember is that it is not always about us.

The story of our hope for resurrection and our acting in faith to bring it about, traveled all over the world. The fact that we did not get a resurrection on this day did not discourage others from taking hope in what may seem like a failure. Rather, it encouraged others to respond in greater faith for their own need.

Shortly after the story I have chronicled here, the church that is connected to our supernatural school in the Philippines was at a community swimming party. One of their children, a 5-year-old girl named Alpha Grace, drowned. They believe she was under the water for over 20-minutes, and when they removed her body from the pool there were no vital signs.

Just five years prior to this drowning, a young boy lost his life in a similar tragedy in this same location and at this same annual event. At this earlier occurrence, the church was not thinking about the possibility of reviving the boy. He was pronounced dead, and they buried him. A family lost their son.

But now, five years later, they were armed with the testimony of our attempt at resurrection, and instead of being resigned to this little girl's death by drowning, they chose hope. They immediately began to pray for her life to be restored. Then they took her lifeless body to a doctor in their small community where she was officially pronounced dead. The doctor was the same man who had pronounced the death of the boy years earlier. Upon seeing

Alpha, he angrily asked, "Why do you keep bringing these dead children to me?"

The mother and friends of Alpha Grace were not deterred, however, and they continued to declare life into her body even as she was being driven by ambulance to the morgue. Suddenly, in the ambulance, little Alpha Grace woke up crying and asking for her mother! This little girl later related the story of how she remembered being in the water and then falling asleep. She told them that while she was sleeping, Jesus came to her and placed an orb of light in each of her hands. The next thing she remembered is waking up in the ambulance and calling for her mom.

It was my privilege later that year to be in the Philippines and meet little Alpha Grace. I watched this energetic, perfectly normal and healthy little girl run around the room where we were having lunch, playing happily with her friends. I will never forget the emotions of the moment when I put my arms around Alpha's father and held the man who had his daughter fully restored to him.

Since Alpha Grace's resurrection, we have witnessed resurrections in Fiji, another one in the Philippines, and even one here in the United States.

Choosing hope is not always just about us.

Endnotes

1. Paraphrased.
2. See Matthew 10:8.

Well… I wish I could describe Him to you…
but He's indescribable. He's indescribable!
That's my King!

—Dr. Shadrach Meshach Lockridge

CHAPTER EIGHT

Hope's

Anchor

I HAVE NEVER SEEN THE MOVIE "Hope Floats," nor do I have any idea what the screenwriter means by the title. However, I am not convinced that hope floats at all. In fact, I am persuaded that hope, to be authentic, must be solidly anchored in something or someone that is trustworthy.

I choose hope because hope comforts me.

Paul, in writing to the Thessalonian Christians, speaks of the difference between grief that opens the door to despair and sorrow that grows a thankful heart and a grateful spirit. The difference is hope.

But I do not want you to be ignorant, brethren, concerning those who have fallen asleep, lest you sorrow as others who have no hope (1 Thessalonians 4:13).

Hope comforts us and helps us see that there is good in the midst and on the other side of our loss.

Since it is the work of the Holy Spirit to come alongside and comfort us, it seems evident that one of the ways He does this is by empowering hope through the distribution of love. I will address this in a later chapter, but for now, consider Paul's words on this subject:

Now hope does not disappoint, because the love of God has been poured out in our hearts by the Holy Spirit who was given to us (Romans 5:5).

Joy Comes in the Mourning

Comfort is often a misunderstood concept. We may believe to give someone comfort is to feel sorry for them in their pain and perhaps put an arm around their shoulder, endorsing their self-pity. This inferior "comfort" leaves us where we are and is not what Holy Spirit gives, nor is it the kind of comfort afforded by hope.

True comfort does not ignore the pain of our situation, but neither does it leave us there. It gives us courage to move on, to get up out of our discouragement and look beyond the difficulty. This is what Holy Spirit does, and this is what hope does.

As I look outside my office door, I can see a large metal sign hanging on the wall of the second-story walkway that stretches across the entranceway of our home. It is cut to form one simple word: joy. It hangs there to remind us of one of hope's comforts.

On the morning after Amy's death, Deborah came down the stairs that lead from our bedroom to the entranceway of our home. As she reached the bottom of the stairs, turned to go down the hall to the living room and reached the place where the walkway crossed over the entrance, Deborah walked right into a tangibly felt yet invisible Presence.

This so caught her by surprise that she stopped moving toward the living room and took a step back, puzzled as to what she had just experienced. After a moment, she stepped forward again, and as before, she ran into the same tangible atmosphere. She stood there for a moment and asked the question, "What is this?"

She then heard the Holy Spirit respond, "This is joy."

I am confident that when Deborah chose hope the day before this experience, declaring that she would not live sad and she would not live mad, it opened the door for the comfort of Holy Spirit through the gift of joy. We discovered that the psalmist was correct when he wrote,

> *Weeping may endure for a night, but joy comes in the morning* (Psalm 30:5).

Though He did not say it this way, we also discovered that weeping may endure for a night, but when we choose hope, joy comes in the mourning.

I choose hope because I belong to the God of all hope.

Hope must be attached to something, otherwise it is

just a wish. Hope, anchored in God, is guaranteed by the character and nature of the One in which one hopes.

The old Lutheran hymn, "The Solid Rock," written by Edward Mote in 1864, continues to powerfully declare the truth of hope's foundation:

> My hope is built on nothing less
> Than Jesus' blood and righteousness;
> I dare not trust the sweetest frame,
> But wholly lean on Jesus' name.
> On Christ, the solid Rock, I stand;
> All other ground is sinking sand.
> When darkness veils His lovely face,
> I rest on His unchanging grace;
> In every high and stormy gale
> My anchor holds within the veil.
> On Christ, the solid Rock, I stand;
> All other ground is sinking sand.

Lesson Learned

Shortly after Deborah and I were married, we learned the truth of a promise is only as good as the one who promises. It was an expensive and hurtful lesson learned the hard way.

Several months before our wedding, I was in an automobile accident caused by a drunk driver. I received a settlement that we determined we would use to build our first home. We found a piece of property in the redwoods outside of Santa Cruz, California, and began looking for a contractor to build our dream home.

We read an advertisement in the newspaper promoting a contractor specializing in constructing homes in the location of our building lot. His name was Gino. We met with Gino and looked at a home he stated was being built by his company. We signed a contract and gave him a deposit. Since I was leaving for a summer ministry internship, Deborah was left to follow-up on the progress.

It was while I was working as a counselor at an Oregon State youth camp that Deborah called with the bad news. Gino had left the area with our deposit along with the deposits of some of the largest contracting companies in the county. Our money was gone, and the sheriff's department did not know where to find Gino.

I remember standing in the Santa Cruz County Sheriff's Office a few weeks later holding the contract in my hand and stating with some confidence, "I have a contract... Surely I will get my money back."

Hope must be attached to something, otherwise it is just a wish.

The sheriff looked at me and said something that felt to me like, "You dumb, naïve, and foolish little boy. That contract is as worthless as a plug nickel. By the time we find Gino, if we ever do, there will be no money to pay your contract or the hundreds of other contracts he has falsified with bigger fish than you up and down this state."

Lesson learned; a contract is only as good as the character of the one who signs it.

My hope is not anchored in Gino or anyone like him. It is connected to the One who signed my contract with His blood and who has guaranteed it with the down payment of His Spirit.

That's My King

A black preacher named Shadrach Meshach Lockridge preached a sermon in the 1970s called, "That's My King." I first heard it when I was a young preacher and was so inspired that I have kept the words all these years. I often pull it out and read it, especially when I need a reminder of how trustworthy and capable my King, my God, and my Savior is. You can now listen online to Reverend Lockridge preach his inspiring message on YouTube, and I highly recommend that you do.

I conclude this chapter and my list of why I choose hope with the text of "That's My King."

> *My King was born King. The Bible says He's a Seven Way King. He's the King of the Jews—that's a Racial King. He's the King of Israel—that's a National King. He's the King of righteousness. He's the King of the ages. He's the King of Heaven. He's the King of glory. He's the King of kings and He is the Lord of lords. Now that's my King.*

> *Well... I wonder if you know Him. Do you know Him? Don't try to mislead me. Do you know my King? David said the heavens declare the glory of God, and the firmament showeth His handiwork. My King is the only one of whom there are no means of measure that can define His limitless love. No farseeing telescope can bring into visibility the coastline of His shoreless supply. No barriers can hinder Him from pouring out His blessing.*

Well... He's enduringly strong. He's entirely sincere. He's eternally steadfast. He's immortally graceful. He's imperially powerful. He's impartially merciful. That's my King! He's God's Son. He's the sinner's Savior. He's the centerpiece of civilization. He stands alone in Himself. He's august. He's unique. He's unparalleled. He's unprecedented. He's supreme. He's pre-eminent.

Well... He's the loftiest idea in literature. He's the highest personality in philosophy. He's the supreme problem in higher criticism. He's the fundamental doctrine of true theology. He's the cardinal necessity of spiritual religion. That's my King! He's the miracle of the age. He's the superlative of everything good that you choose to call Him.

Well... He's the only One able to supply all of our needs simultaneously. He supplies strength for the weak. He's available for the tempted and the tried. He sympathizes and He saves. He guards and He guides. He heals the sick. He cleansed the lepers. He forgives sinners. He discharges debtors. He delivers the captives. He defends the feeble. He blesses the young. He serves the unfortunate. He regards the aged. He rewards the diligent and He beautifies the meek. Do you know Him?

Well... my King is a King of knowledge. He's the wellspring of wisdom. He's the doorway of deliverance. He's the pathway of peace.

He's the roadway of righteousness. He's the highway of holiness. He's the gateway of glory. He's the master of the mighty. He's the captain of the conquerors. He's the head of the heroes. He's the leader of the legislatures. He's the overseer of the over-comers. He's the governor of governors. He's the prince of princes. He's the King of kings and He's the Lord of lords. That's my King! That's my King! His office is manifold. His promise is sure. His light is matchless. His goodness is limitless. His mercy is everlasting. His love never changes. His Word is enough. His grace is sufficient. His reign is righteous. His yoke is easy and His burden is light.

Well... I wish I could describe Him to you... but He's indescribable. He's indescribable! That's my King! He's incomprehensible, He's invincible, and He is irresistible. I'm coming to tell you this, that the heavens of heavens cannot contain Him, let alone a man explain Him. You can't get Him out of your mind. You can't get Him off of your hands. You can't outlive Him and you can't live without Him.

Well... the Pharisees couldn't stand Him, but they found out they couldn't stop Him. Pilate couldn't find any fault in Him. The witnesses couldn't get their testimonies to agree. Herod couldn't kill Him. Death couldn't handle Him and the grave couldn't hold Him. That's my King! Yeah!

He always has been and He always will be. I'm talking about He had no predecessor and He'll have no successor. There was nobody before Him and there'll be nobody after Him. You can't impeach Him and He's not going to resign. That's my King! That's my King! Thine is the kingdom and the power and the glory.

Well... All the power belongs to my King. We're around here talking about black power and white power and green power, but it's GOD's power! Thine is the power. Yeah! And the glory. We try to get prestige and honor and glory for ourselves, but the glory is all His. Yes! Thine is the Kingdom and the power and the glory, forever and ever and ever and ever. How long is that? And ever and ever and ever and ever... And when you get through with all of the forevers, then... Amen!

You will see what you look for,
and you will find what you seek.

—Ivan Tait

CHAPTER NINE

H.O.P.E.

"IS SHE GONE?"

"Yes."

This was the brief exchange between Deborah and me on Saturday, June 20, 2009, the day before Father's Day.

It had never occurred to me that I would ever have to ask that question or hear that answer. Outliving my child is not what is supposed to happen. I'm the parent that watches his child grow up, have children, and one day I leave and they live on. That is how it's meant to be. Yet, here I was standing in a small room of the emergency wing of the hospital with Deborah and the lifeless body of our thirty-one-year-old daughter.

Keeping Hope Alive

I was an hour away from home, enjoying a day with my eldest son, Jeremy, when I received the call informing me that paramedics were rushing Amy to the nearby hospital from our home where she had suddenly collapsed in Deborah's arms. The caller tearfully conveyed to me that the prognosis was not good and that I should come home as quickly as possible. Though I don't remember much about that ride from Infineon Raceway to North Bay Hospital, I do recall the vicious assault on my hope.

The battle to keep hope alive did not improve when I saw the downcast faces of dear friends standing in the hall of the hospital wiping the tears from their faces. When I stepped into that eight-by-eight cubical where the doctors and nurses had so diligently and passionately attempted to revive my daughter, hope of a positive outcome was crushed.

There was Deborah sitting with her arm stretched over Amy quietly weeping.

"Is she gone?" I asked, not wanting to hear what I feared her answer to be.

"Yes," Deborah tearfully replied.

It was in the death of the hope that Amy would live that a new perspective on hope began to take shape in my thinking. *If hope is one of the big three (faith, hope, and love) that remain forever when everything else does not, then where is hope hiding in this circumstance?* It was curious to me that although my hope of Amy's life was gone, I still had hope. *How can that be? What is keeping my hope alive?*

Since that day in June, I often find myself chewing on these kinds of questions, sometimes even finding answers. On one such occasion the letters of the word "hope" began to form the acrostic "H.O.P.E."—Holding Our Perspective Eternal.

H — Holding

There was a time in the life of Joshua, the protégé of Moses and the eventual great leader of Israel, that tenacity was the essential ingredient to success. Moses, the man who had been his mentor, leader, and spiritual guide, was dead, and the reins of leadership were now in Joshua's hands. It was his responsibility to transition the nation from forty years of wandering in the wilderness to entering and possessing a promised land. The challenge was massive, and the stakes were high.

It was in this moment that Joshua received his instruction from God. We find it recorded in Joshua chapter one.

> *Moses My servant is dead. Now therefore, arise, go over this Jordan, you and all this people, to the land which I am giving to them... so I will be with you. I will not leave you nor forsake you* (vs. 2, 5).

Following this directive and promise, God tells Joshua,

> *Be strong and of good courage...* (v. 6).

He repeats this three times but with an added emphasis on the final repetition:

> *Have I not commanded you? Be strong and of good courage...* (v. 9).

105

The word "strong" is translated from the Hebrew word *chazaq*, and "good courage" is translated from the Hebrew word *amats*. Chazaq means, "to prevail, to take hold of with strength." Amats means, "to be determined, persistent, to exhibit strength." Together we get this word picture of one who grabs hold of something and refuses to let go. In Joshua's case, God commands him to apprehend and tenaciously hold onto three things: God's promises, God's instructions, and God's presence.

While vacationing with my sister and her family in a houseboat on the California Delta, my son Ryan taught me a lesson regarding tenacity. We had rented a ski boat and were enjoying both skiing and kneeboarding. Ryan was about twelve-years-old at the time and was not interested in skiing but wanted to learn how to kneeboard. It was presenting quite a challenge for him.

As you may know, a kneeboard is a small board pulled behind a boat with the rider hanging onto the towrope and kneeling on knee-shaped depressions in the top of the board. The challenge in this sport is making the transition from lying on the board to kneeling on the board as the boat accelerates to towing speed. Accomplishing this maneuver is the difference between being dragged through the water and riding on the surface. It was this transition that Ryan was finding difficult.

Attempt after attempt, Ryan would plow through the water half-submerged, trying to get his knees up onto the board, and time after time he would fail. The astonishing thing was that he never let go of the towrope. No matter how long we kept accelerating, and regardless of how submerged he became, he tenaciously held onto the rope. Those of us in the boat would finally have to call a halt to the process and let him rest so he could try again. Finally, he mastered the transition and enjoyed the ride.

H.O.P.E.

Living in hope requires tenacity, an unwillingness to let go no matter how deep we are in the circumstances of life. It requires apprehending the promises and holding on for the long haul, seeing the journey through the lens of hope.

O — Our

I know I have said this before, but allow me to emphasize it here once again: this journey of hope is personal. Though we can be encouraged in hope through the testimony of others, at the end of the day, it must be our perspective, our hope. Others cannot apprehend it or hold on for us. We alone must decide to choose the option to be strong and courageous, to grab ahold of hope and refuse to release it. I have heard it said, "Hope never abandons you; you abandon hope," and I believe this to be true.

One of the great challenges of our time in western culture is the threat of the entitlement mentality. It is my observation that our present generation increasingly believes it is entitled to have certain things handed to them without taking personal responsibility. "It's not my fault," and, "There's nothing I can do about it," are examples of the attitude that manifest this mentality. If this trend continues, I believe we will be a people that has lost the ability to apprehend a thing and make it our own.

Bum Philips, the former coach of the NFL football team formerly known as the Houston Oilers, made this insightful observation:

> *You can fail all the time, but you're not a failure until you start blaming someone else.*

Blaming others or our circumstances for our negative perspective or our lack of hope is the road to true failure.

The road to a greater reality starts by taking ownership of our choices.

P — Perspective

Perspective is our point of view, the lens through which we see things. Our perspective will determine our conclusions, and our conclusions will determine our actions, and ultimately, our results.

Instant replay in sporting events gives us a good understanding of the importance of perspective. When we watch a football play live, for example, and we see the ball come loose from the player's hand, our first conclusion may be that the player fumbled the ball. It is the only conclusion to come to because that is what we see from our limited view. If this were the only perspective of the referee, he would award the football to the team that recovered the ball.

However, when we see this same play as it is recorded by one of the many cameras positioned around the playing field, we have a different perspective and may come to a very different conclusion. From this new vantage point, we see that the player's knee was on the ground before he lost control of the ball and that it was actually not a fumble at all. With this perspective, the referee would allow the offensive team to retain control of the football.

Choosing our perspective is imperative to keeping us living in hope. If we see our life experiences and challenges from the wrong point of view, we will find ourselves coming to the wrong conclusions and making incorrect decisions that will defeat our destiny.

H.O.P.E.

During the long drive to the hospital that day before Father's Day, I never ceased declaring the Scriptures, praying for the defeat of the spirit of death, and prophesying Amy's destiny. It was with a high level of faith coupled with the hope that I was not arriving too late—that Amy was still alive and that she would recover. With this high level of faith and hope I exited my car and entered the hospital emergency room.

As you can imagine, I was stunned a few moments later as I stood looking down at Deborah, with her arm draped over the lifeless body of my daughter. I had done all I knew to do, and still, she was gone. That picture is forever imprinted on my memory, and I cannot change the reality of that moment. What I can change, however, is the perspective from which I choose to see that moment and from which I view the many months of grieving my loss that followed.

E — Eternal

An eternal perspective is one that sees all of life in light of the long term. Knowing that I will see my daughter again is a very real and tangible hope that affects me every day. It is an eternal perspective that not only cheers me, but motivates me. The perspective that comes from the hope of life after death is vital to living in hope.

Beyond this blessed hope, having an eternal perspective is also having this point of view—

> *And we know that all things work together for good to those who love God, to those who are called according to His purpose* (Romans 8:28).

It is much more than simply relegating everything good to Heaven.

109

On one of my long flights back from Fiji, I took some time to have a conversation with God. I had been contemplating several issues and decided to ask Him about His perspective on loss and failure. His initial response surprised me. "I want to first tell you how much you mean to Me." His primary response to my question did not have to do with loss or failure, but rather, how He saw me in the midst of my loss and failure.

He went on to speak of my value to Him and His absolute commitment to me in every season of my life, whether in times of success, failure, loss or gain. He made it clear that He does not see me in light of these things, but in light of His love for me. This revelation rocked my world.

His second response was equally surprising and revelatory. He reminded me of the verse out of Romans that I just referred to and then impressed on me the following:

> *Every loss and failure is the fertilizer that will give nutrition to the soil of your next harvest. They are either the septic poison that will kill your future, or they will be the nutrients for your future prosperity. The key to which one it will be is your response to failure and loss in light of who I am and what I have promised.*

"All things work together for good." This, I believe, is an eternal perspective. God cannot allow any of the things we go through to go to waste. He always makes them to be for the benefit of those who walk and co-labor with Him for the working out of His will in all these things.

So then, every loss, failure, success, hurt, joy, relationship, pain, sorrow, experience, circumstance— everything—must work for my good. All of life can be made only to serve my advancement and the establishment of my destiny. Everything must bow to my good. My progress is not prisoner to my circumstance but my loss and failure are servants to my destiny.

You may be thinking that your present negative circumstance is working against you, but the truth is, it is working on your behalf.

> *For our light and momentary troubles are achieving for us an eternal glory that far outweighs them all. So we fix our eyes not on what is seen, but on what is unseen, since what is seen is temporary, but what is unseen is eternal* (2 Corinthians 4:17-18, NIV).

An eternal perspective is accessible to us through our heavenly position. Paul states it clearly in Ephesians 2:

> *And God raised us up with Christ and seated us with him in the heavenly realms in Christ Jesus* (v. 6, NIV).

Because of this position, we can view all of life from above which allows us a perspective not under the influence and control of our earthly circumstances. Living in heavenly places in Christ should have us living from eternity with a perspective that is larger than the moment.

An eternal perspective is looking both ways—what is behind us and what is in front of us—from a vantage point that empowers what is around us.

This perspective is—

- Drawing on our inheritance—knowing that we are part of something that was;

- Living in our destiny—knowing we are part of something that now is; and

- Looking to our legacy—knowing we are part of something that is to come.

When we were born into the kingdom of God, we took on a new ancestry and acquired a new inheritance.

> *The Spirit you received does not make you slaves, so that you live in fear again; rather, the Spirit you received brought about your adoption to sonship. And by him we cry, "Abba, Father." The Spirit himself testifies with our spirit that we are God's children. Now if we are children, then we are heirs—heirs of God and co-heirs with Christ, if indeed we share in his sufferings in order that we may also share in his glory* (Romans 8:15-17, NIV).

This adoption into sonship changes everything.

> *Therefore, if anyone is in Christ, he is a new creation; old things have passed away; behold, all things have become new* (2 Corinthians 5:17).

Royal Lineage

No matter what your earthly ancestry was like, you now are of a different lineage.

When I was a kid, I was impressed when one of my

friends said, "I can trace my family back to the Queen of England." That no longer impresses me. I can trace my family back to the King of kings, Abraham, the father of nations, Moses the deliverer, Deborah the judge, King David, Queen Esther, the Apostles Paul, John, and Peter. All of these are now my family.

It gets even better; their victories and breakthroughs are now mine also. Their history with God is an open door for me to walk through and is now part of my history.

My progress is not prisoner to my circumstance, but my loss and failure are servants to my destiny.

In the movie, "Walk in the Clouds," a young man returning from World War II is thrust into a family with rich Spanish heritage when he agrees to pretend to be married to the family's daughter. Having been raised in an orphanage, his own family history is not known. The father of the family is not pleased with the thought of this new son-in-law with no heritage and treats him as an outcast.

At the end of the movie, the father experiences a major crisis. When he discovers that his daughter and her "husband" have deceived him regarding their relationship, he reacts with a violent outburst of anger. His actions result in the family vineyard being set ablaze. Though the family fights valiantly to save it, the vineyard is completely destroyed.

As the family is sitting in the burned-out remains of the vineyard, stunned by the destruction around them, the young man remembered that the grandfather had shown him the original vine the vineyard had come from. He momentarily slips away from the family and goes out to see if the original vine survived the fire disaster.

Soon he returns to the family with a cutting from the root of the original vine and hands it to the father, inquiring, "Is it still alive?"

The father cuts into the root and with tearful relief acknowledges that it is indeed alive. The father then turns to the young man who wants to marry his daughter and holds the root in front of him, passionately declaring, "This is now your root, your history, your family, your inheritance."

With this act the father was announcing to this young orphan, "Welcome to the family. You now have a new family along with a new history, heritage, and future.

We are a part of what was, what is, and what will be. Steven Fry, author, pastor, and composer writes:

We are the fruit of an ancient prayer.

We now hold a baton that has been passed down to us, and those who have passed it to us—our ancestors—are in the stands cheering us on to continue courageously and complete the race victoriously.

> *Therefore we also, since we are surrounded by so great a cloud of witnesses... let us run with endurance the race that is set before us* (Hebrews 12:1).

We are the history of the next generation, and we influence the future from our place in their history. As we have drawn on the lives of those who have come before us, those that follow will draw on ours. What we are will be part of what will be.

We stand in our present, between the generations before us and the generations that will follow, Holding Our Perspective Eternal.

Hope itself is like a star—not to be seen in the sunshine of prosperity, and only to be discovered in the night of adversity.

—Charles H. Spurgeon

CHAPTER TEN

Abundant

Hope

ABUNDANT HOPE IS THE ENEMY of hope's enemies. The assault on hope must be met with hope—not an anemic thin thread of hope, but hope in abundance.

We live in a time when hope is being attacked from every arena of our world. Continuing to have hope for our political process, our economic recovery, or lasting peace in the nations is becoming more difficult every day. It does not help that news stories of hopeless situations are reported 24-hours a day through a variety of news sources. Negativity bombards our senses and defies our optimism.

This is nothing new. Every generation has its challenges

and must combat hope's enemies. In my father's generation they faced the despair of the Great Depression in the 1930s along with the devastation of World War II. The assault in our generation may look different, but it can be just as consuming. We must realize that we have an enemy who goes about "like a roaring lion, seeking whom he may devour."[1] I am convinced that hope is one of his favorite meals.

This assault on hope must be met with an abundant, outrageous, supercharged-hope.

The good news is that we have a hope supercharger living in us.

> *Now may the God of hope fill you with all joy and peace in believing, that you may abound in hope by the power of the Holy Spirit* (Romans 15:13).

I love this verse in the Amplified version:

> *May the God of your hope so fill you with all joy and peace in believing [through the experience of your faith] that by the power of the Holy Spirit you may abound and be overflowing (bubbling over) with hope* (AMP).

The word in Romans 15:13 translated "abound" is the Greek word *perisseuo.* It means to "super abound, to excel" in both quality and quantity, to "be in excess." In other words, to have "more than enough." The Holy Spirit is the One who causes our hope to be turbo-charged, to be "more than enough." He is our hope accelerator.

Living with supercharged, over-the-top hope comes

through our partnership with the One who lives in us, and who is not, in any way, limited in hope. He does not live or give out of a budget, but He is the One who is exceedingly, abundantly above all we could ask or think. In Him we do not have to choose hope level A, B, or C. We can have the whole alphabet.

Bill Johnson states:

> *Any situation that is without hope is living under the influence of a lie.*

Jesus said He would send Holy Spirit and that He would lead and guide us into all truth. We don't have to live under the lie of lack or hopelessness. We can live in the truth of the Holy Spirit's power to take us from anemic hope into heavenly realms of abundant hope.

Jeremiah's Lament

The Prophet Jeremiah was called "the weeping prophet" for a reason. He lived in the time when he had to watch his nation disintegrate and slide into captivity, in spite of his warnings. He endured hurtful persecution by the very people he was trying to help, and except for the compassion of one of the court eunuchs, Jeremiah would have died in prison, falsely accused of treason. He wept for his nation; he wept for his own condition.

Jeremiah records his weeping—his lament—in the book appropriately named, Lamentations. The book begins:

> *How lonely sits the city that was full of people! How like a widow is she, who was great among the nations! The princess among the provinces has become a slave!* (1:1)

He continues,

> *She weeps bitterly in the night, her tears are on her cheeks; among all her lovers she has none to comfort her. All her friends have dealt treacherously with her; they have become her enemies* (v. 2).

By the time we read into the third chapter, the prophet Jeremiah has gone from mourning his nation's plight to lamenting his own.

> *I am the man who has seen affliction by the rod of His wrath. He has led me and made me walk in darkness and not in light.* (3:1-2).

His description darkens as we read on.

> *He has broken my teeth with gravel; he has trampled me in the dust. I have been deprived of peace; I have forgotten what prosperity is. So I say, "My splendor is gone and all that I had hoped from the LORD." I remember my affliction and my wandering, the bitterness and the gall. I well remember them, and my soul is downcast within me* (vs. 16-20).

This is the cry of a man about to abandon hope. Yet in the middle of all this depressing reality, something happens in the heart and mind of Jeremiah. In his next expression, we find several keys to living in an abundant, supercharged hope. He records his transition from despair to hope this way:

> *Yet this I call to mind and therefore I have*

hope: Because of the LORD'S great love we are not consumed, for his compassions never fail. They are new every morning; great is your faithfulness. I say to myself, "The LORD is my portion; therefore I will wait for him." The LORD is good to those whose hope is in him, to the one who seeks him (3:21-26, NIV).

In reading this passage, you can almost feel a fresh wind of encouragement blow across the page as Jeremiah makes a shift in his thinking. His perspective changes and the caustic, negative atmosphere is overturned.

Several years ago a reporter interviewed a former member of my staff, and the article was printed in the local newspaper. This staff person had been laid off several months' prior to the interview and was, at the time of the interview, still being paid severance by the church. In the article, the former staff member inferred some very negative things about the church and about me personally.

When I read the article, I was angry and wounded. Criticism never feels good, but this was unfair and especially hurtful. I am confident that there are many valid criticisms of my leadership over 40-plus years, but the criticism in this article was not of that sort. All that day my mind was filled with unhealthy thoughts and vain imaginations.

As it was nearing the evening that same day, the Holy Spirit finally broke through my darkness and reminded me of something better to think about. He took me to Jesus' words recorded in Matthew chapter 5:

Blessed are you when they revile and persecute you, and say all kinds of evil against you falsely for My sake. Rejoice and be exceedingly glad, for great is your reward in heaven... (vs. 11-12).

An amazing thing happened almost immediately. When I chose to think on this verse, my whole world changed. Instead of bordering on depression, I was excited and encouraged. This man's actions had made a deposit in my reward account in Heaven. I wasn't losing; I was winning. I yelled out loud, "Hit me again! I could use more reward!"

Jeremiah's Secrets to Choosing Hope

As we read through Jeremiah's transformed lament, we see several things that He chooses to bring to mind, each of them providing fresh fuel for his hope.

The first thing we notice is that he recalls the true nature of God. Jeremiah begins to dwell on the fact that God is compassionate, loving, and faithful. He ties his mind to the nature and character of God and thereby energizes his hope.

When we come to those places where normal reason cannot give us adequate answers, we can either live in the confusion and despair or put our minds on what we know about the goodness and character of God. When we recall His nature, the Holy Spirit—whose job it is to lead us into the truth—increases our revelation, and our hope levels accelerate.

The second hope accelerator for Jeremiah is that he recalls to his mind, not only the character of God, but also the effectiveness of God's character and nature. The Amplified version states it this way:

It is because of the LORD'S mercy and loving-

kindness that we are not consumed, because His tender compassions fail not. They are new every morning; great and abundant is Your stability and faithfulness (Lamentations 3:22-23, AMP).

God is not only merciful, His mercies are the very reason I am not consumed by all the stuff that is swirling around me trying to steal my life. He is not only compassionate, His compassions do not fail—they never wear out, and they don't give up. In fact, they renew themselves in their effectiveness every single morning.

Wow! His mercy and His compassion will extend beyond my present crises, and my circumstances will not wear out His benevolence. He is more than enough in both quantity and quality.

When we recall all of this, hope lives abundantly!

Jeremiah next releases hope by recalling his personal history with God. When he declared, "Great is Your faithfulness," he was not just referring to a theological concept, but rather, connecting the concept with specific experiences that testify to the truth of it for him.

One of those experiences in Jeremiah's history with God took place just prior to the captivity of Israel. Jeremiah knew that Israel had broken covenant with God, and therefore, God had instructed him to prophesy 70 years of captivity. Yet in the midst of impending judgment, God promises full restoration of the nation and gives Jeremiah instruction to perform a prophetic act to illustrate His intent.

Jeremiah, following God's instruction, bought a field from his cousin, prepared and signed the deed among witnesses, put a seal on it, and placed it in a clay jar in order to preserve it. He then made this public declaration:

> For thus says the LORD of hosts, the God of Israel: "Houses and fields and vineyards shall be possessed again in this land" (32:15).

I love the way Scripture does not hide the humanity of its heroes. After fulfilling God's instructions and announcing the prophetic word of the Lord promising the redemption of the people and the Land, Jeremiah questions God's sanity. Here is my personal amplified version of this section.

> Oh Lord God, have You lost Your mind? You birth a mighty nation through Your great power. You establish them in their own Land and tell them to obey Your ways. They do not follow Your instruction, so You had me prophesy calamity and captivity, which, by the way, God, in case You haven't noticed, has happened. And now, in spite of the fact that the city has been given into the hand of the Chaldeans, You have me buy captured land and do it in front of witnesses so my foolishness is public. What is this all about? [2]

In the next several verses God explains to Jeremiah His heart: to restore His people back to the Land.

> Behold, I will gather them out of all countries where I have driven them... Yes, I will rejoice over them to do them good, and I will assuredly plant them in this land... And fields will be bought in this land... Men will buy fields for

money, sign deeds and seal them... (vs. 37, 41,
43-44).

I am confident that this experience is part of Jeremiah's
personal history in God and part of his thinking when he
declares, "great is Your faithfulness."

When we take what we know the Scripture says about
God and connect it with our personal history and then
bring that into our present situation, hope erupts and is
nurtured. Failing to do so causes our hope to become a
religious concept, losing all of its power.

It is often while speaking in other churches, I will
hear a leader shout out to the congregation, "God is good..." with the expected response, "...all the time." Though I am convinced this is true, I often wonder how many of those responding with such enthusiasm have made the connection between the concept and

We've got God, and He's got us. It can't get any better than that.

I

the reality. Do they have a context in which to deposit
their belief, or is their expression simply wishful thinking?

When I declare, "God is good," I am speaking from my
personal history in God. For me, God is good because as
we buried our daughter, His presence sustained us, kept
us, comforted us, held us, and gave us joy in a joyless
circumstance. Now, in each new crisis, I draw on this
history, and hope is nurtured and empowered.

When I proclaim, "God is Jehovah Jireh, my provider,"
I am not just quoting Scripture; I am drawing on
several true, life experiences in God. I am calling up

the miraculous provision of over $3.8 million dollars to build our sanctuary. I draw on the fact that one day we were faced with closing down the sanctuary building project because we had no money to continue, but the very next day we had $800,000 deposited in our account from an unexpected source. And just a few weeks later, the remaining $400,000 came in, and we were able to complete the project!

I recall the critical need for $35,000 in personal funds to provide for my family and how God gave Deborah and I a word of wisdom that became the strategy to provide those funds. Now, with every need presented, hope becomes my default because I call to mind my history in God.

Make it Personal

You may be saying, "I don't have any history in God like you do." Well, get one. I'm not kidding. Take the promises in Scripture and believe them enough to test them out in practical ways in your life. Move from expectation to anticipation—which I'll talk more about in the next chapter. Then your breakthroughs will become your history, and your history will be a source to supercharge your hope.

What are you recalling? What are you pulling up into your thinking from your memory banks? What are you choosing to think about and chew on? This choice is critical; it has the power to determine your level of hope.

Here's an exercise: why not use Facebook as "hope book." Where it is often used to sound off negative and useless thoughts, consider its greater potential as a forum for increasing and nurturing hope. How about using it as a personal "testimony book" declaring the goodness of God through the many ways He intervened in your life? Why not turn it into an opportunity to reveal the character and nature of God and post a status about His faithfulness?

In Lamentations 3:24 Jeremiah proclaims what I believe to be the number one key to having abundant, life-giving hope.

> *"The* LORD *is my portion," says my soul, "therefore hope in Him!"*

Jeremiah is recalling that God is his true inheritance, and in doing so, his hope is renewed. "I have all these nations around me boasting of their power, their wealth, their history, but Jehovah—the One superior in quality and quantity—is my portion."

Hope is not just sustained, but rather, it increases in potency when we recall the One to whom we really belong and who it is that has promised to belong to us. We've got God, and He's got us. It can't get any better than that. When we live in this reality, our cry can then be like David's:

> *Some trust in chariots, and some in horses; but we will remember the name of the* LORD *our God. They have bowed down and fallen; but we have risen and stand upright* (Psalm 20:7-8).

I want to finish this chapter with again looking to Romans 4:18-21. Let your hope increase as you read Paul's narrative.

When everything was hopeless, Abraham believed anyway, deciding to live not on the basis of what he saw he couldn't do but on what God said he would do. And so he was made father of a multitude of peoples. God himself said to him, "You're going to have a big family, Abraham!"

> *Abraham didn't focus on his own impotence and say, "It's hopeless. This hundred-year-old body could never father a child." Nor did he survey Sarah's decades of infertility and give up. He didn't tiptoe around God's promise asking cautiously skeptical questions. He plunged into the promise and came up strong, ready for God, sure that God would make good on what he had said* (THE MESSAGE).

Endnotes

1. See 1 Peter 5:8.
2. Author's paraphrase based on Jeremiah 32:16-25.

Faith goes up the stairs that love has built and looks out the windows which hope has opened.

—Charles H. Spurgeon

CHAPTER ELEVEN

Faith, Hope, and Love

Paul MAKES AN INTERESTING, if not arresting, statement in 1 Corinthians 13:

> *And now abide faith, hope, love, these three...*
> (v. 13).

The word "abide" refers to the qualities of endurance, continuity, and sustained Presence. Since Paul places these three together as qualities that will remain constant, it might be good to look at the connection between them. Since hope stands between the other two, it seems especially interesting to me to explore hope's relationship to faith and love.

The Faith Connection

Faith is the evidence that we hope; therefore, hope is the father of faith. Abraham believed while standing in hope, the seedbed of faith: "Contrary to hope, in hope believed." Hope defeats doubt, allowing faith to grow. Hope is our context; faith is our response.

I was flying at about 33,000 feet returning from our supernatural school in the Philippines when I believe I heard the Holy Spirit say, "It's time to move from expectation to anticipation—to add faith to your hope." This brief instruction set me on a journey of discovering what this could mean.

Expectation is the essence of hope. When we hope, we are setting our focus with confident expectation that we will receive, or see, that for which we are hoping.

Anticipation is an essential element of faith. Anticipation is an awareness of an imminent realization that positions us for what is coming. When we act in faith, we are not just focusing on what we are hoping for, but we are moving in anticipation so that we are positioned to receive what we are expecting.

I have played racquetball off and on for over 40 years. In the last several years, I have been competing against men younger, faster, and stronger than me. The only reason I am able to stay on the court without embarrassing myself is by maintaining a consistent level of anticipation. I not only expect the opponent to hit the ball, but I move according to where I anticipate the ball is going.

Expectation sets our focus; anticipation moves us to act in preparation. To live in expectation without acting in anticipation leaves us unprepared to receive the very thing we are hoping for.

Faith, Hope, and Love

Jesus illustrated this with the parable of the ten virgins.

> *Then the kingdom of heaven shall be likened to ten virgins who took their lamps and went out to meet the bridegroom. Now five of them were wise, and five were foolish. Those who were foolish took their lamps and took no oil with them, but the wise took oil in their vessels with their lamps* (Matthew 25:1-4).

The virgins that Jesus is referring to in this parable are those whose duty it was to attend the bride with lamps. They were to be ready at the appearance of the bridegroom to conduct the bride to his house and go in with him to the wedding. All of the virgins in this parable expected the bridegroom to come and looked forward to attending the bride. Both the wise and the foolish virgins took their lamps filled with oil, but only the wise took extra oil, anticipating a time of delay.

When the coming of the bridegroom was announced, the wise virgins, were ready to attend the bride, receive the bridegroom, and go into the wedding. The foolish virgins however, realized they did not have enough oil and had to go purchase more. They expected but did not anticipate; they hoped but failed to act in faith. Matthew records the result:

> *But while they were on their way to buy the oil, the bridegroom arrived. The virgins who were ready went in with him to the wedding banquet. And the door was shut. Later the others also came. "Lord, Lord," they said, "open the door for us!" But he replied, "Truly I tell you, I don't know you"* (Matthew 25:10-12, NIV).

The early development and usage of our English word "to anticipate" gives us further insight into what I believe the Holy Spirit is teaching us. Its early usage is found around 1530 and meant, "to cause to happen sooner."[1] As we live in expectation (hope) and move in anticipation (faith) we are in position to attract and receive the very thing we hope for.

Accelerated Realities

Could it be that our anticipation actually accelerates the coming of the thing expected? I believe that what I call the "suddenlies" of God—the swift fulfillment of God's promises—are, in part, the result of our moving in anticipation to receive. I am equally convinced that our failure to anticipate is, in part, the reason for the delay of that fulfillment.

Three kings—Jehoram, the king of Israel, Jehoshaphat, king of Judah, and the unnamed king of Edom—marched against the rebellious king of Moab. After marching for seven days, their troops were tired and thirsty, for there was no water for the army. Jehoram was quick to declare defeat, but Jehoshaphat was ready with a suggestion that they inquire of the prophet Elisha as to what to do to solve the problem. Elisha, after hearing the word of the Lord, spoke it to the three kings:

> *Make this valley full of ditches. For, thus says the LORD: "You shall not see wind, nor shall you see rain; yet that valley shall be filled with water, so that you, your cattle, and your animals may drink." And this is a simple matter in the sight of the LORD; He will also deliver the Moabites into your hand* (2 Kings 3:16-18).

Faith, Hope, and Love

These three kings now had the hope of a promise from God. They expected Him to act on their behalf. However, the fulfillment of that promise required that they act in anticipation to dig ditches for water that was not evident. This meant that tired, thirsty troops would have to dig dry, dusty trenches all along the landscape in the heat of the day to prepare for what they could not see.

The kings chose to stand in hope and move in faith by digging the ditches. The deep ditches drew in and held the sudden rush of water that came in the morning, not only providing the necessary refreshment for the army but becoming the basis for a trap that brought about the destruction of the Moabite army.

Would the water have come anyway if they had not dug the trenches? Maybe, maybe not. But in any case, without the ditches, they would not have preserved the water for the troops, and there would have been no victory over their enemy.

Hope allows us to believe, and therefore, move in faith one more time, even when our history would dictate otherwise. This is the picture that is recorded in the Gospel of Luke. Peter fished all night and yet caught no fish. Even so, Jesus asked him to go out once again and fish— at the least likely time of day. This was an unreasonable request, and yet Jesus' words to him sparked hope in Peter, and so he responded in an unreasonable way. Peter believed one more time and acted in faith:

> *Nevertheless* [in spite of my recent futile attempt] *at Your word I will let down the net* (author's comments).

The result of Peter's unreasonable response, sparked by hope, was an unreasonable catch:

When they had done this, they caught a great number of fish, and their net was breaking. So they signaled to their partners in the other boat to come and help them. And they came and filled both the boats, so that they began to sink (vs. 6-7).

Hope and faith are two unreasonable partners working together to bring about promises fulfilled.

The Love Connection

Love empowers and authenticates hope.

Now hope does not disappoint, because the love of God has been poured out in our hearts by the Holy Spirit who was given to us (Romans 5:5).

The love of God guarantees that our hope placed in Him will not leave us deceived or ashamed.

I hate to admit it, but Deborah and I are creatures of habit, especially when it comes to our arrival on the Island of Maui twice each year. After claiming our luggage from the airport carousel and driving our rental car to the opposite side of the island, we first stop at Sargent's Fine Art Gallery in the picturesque town of Lahaina to drop off Deborah's paintings. We then walk along Front Street until we come to the stairs leading up to one of our favorite places to eat, Lahaina Pizza Company. We need not look at the menu for our choices will always be the same on our first day on Maui: tropical iced tea, hot buffalo wings, and bruschetta.

Recently, while following this routine and enjoying our selections, I made the comment to Deborah, "This bruschetta is just as good as I remembered. It never disappoints." We discussed how this could be possible and came to the conclusion that it was all about the quality and consistency of the ingredients.

If you have ever tasted Maui onions and Maui tomatoes you know what I mean. The soil they are grown in and the quantity of moisture they receive as they mature results in the sweetest and most flavorful produce anywhere. The bruschetta never disappoints because the ingredients are consistently incomparable.

What does this have to do with hope and love? Simply this, hope does not disappoint because of the quality of love that is distributed into our lives by the Holy Spirit. Hope swims in a pool of love that is unconditional, unparalleled, incomparable, and unlimited. Hope is validated, not only by the God that loves us, but also by the God that is love. Love is His very essence; it is who He is not just what He does. This guarantees the quality of His love and empowers hope.

The Apostle Paul, when writing to the church in Ephesus expressed his desire:

> *And I pray that you, being rooted and established in love, may have power, together with all the Lord's holy people, to grasp how wide and long and high and deep is the love of Christ, and to know this love that surpasses knowledge— that you may be filled to the measure of all the fullness of God* (Ephesians 3:17-19, NIV).

Our hope will not abandon us because we are loved by the One whose love is deep enough to reach down to us in the time of our greatest failure or loss and restore us. Our hope will not be inadequate because the One whose love is wide enough to embrace anyone and bring him or her into right relationship, loves us.

We will not be disappointed in hope because His love is high enough to draw us into heavenly realms of glory so that we are seated in heavenly places with Christ. We will never be disillusioned in hope because His love is long enough, stretching out into our future with no possible end. His love stands behind our hope and gives it potency.

No wonder Paul prayed with such passion that we would be able to "grasp" the dimensions of God's love. The word "grasp" means, "to lay hold of so as to possess as one's own; to appropriate."[3]

In 1917 Frederick Lehman wrote the powerful song, "The Love of God." The third verse to that song, however, was written anonymously and found penciled on the wall of an insane asylum after the patient that had occupied the room died. It speaks of the kind of love that makes one a prisoner of hope.

> Could we with ink the ocean fill,
> And were the skies of parchment made,
> Were every stalk on earth a quill,
> And every man a scribe by trade,
> To write the love of God above,
> Would drain the ocean dry.
> Nor could the scroll contain the whole,
> Though stretched from sky to sky.
>
> Oh, love of God, how rich and pure!
> How measureless and strong!
> It shall forever more endure
> The saints' and angels' song.

Hopelessness Defeated By Unreasonable Love

During one of my times of deep grief in which I felt overwhelmed and on the edge of despair, the Holy Spirit reminded me of a technique I use when SCUBA diving to dispel the feeling of panic. As I recounted in an earlier chapter, my first experiences in diving had moments of panic caused by feeling like I could not breathe.

In spite of this bad experience, I was determined to discover the joy of SCUBA and knew there had to be a way to overcome the negative feelings. It was almost by accident that I discovered as I began to focus on the picturesque world around me—the color of the light coming through the water, the varied shapes and sizes of coral, and the beautiful tropical fish—I was distracted from measuring every breath and would begin to relax.

Expectation sets our focus; anticipation moves us to act in preparation.

In using this technique, SCUBA no longer disappointed and a whole new world opened to me.

The Holy Spirit encouraged me to use this same technique to overcome the panic of hopelessness. He said to focus my attention on Him and the qualities of the love with which He loves me. This was best done for me through worship. When I began to do this, I was not only distracted from my grief, I was enveloped in His love and filled with fresh, effective hope.

The love of God is unreasonable. John tried to describe it by saying, "God so loved..." That one little word, "so," is far bigger than most of us realize. He sooooooooo loved us. He so unreasonably loved us that He emptied Heaven of its greatest treasure in order to purchase the lives of those who had rebelled against Him and deserved death. That kind of love is unreasonable.

It seems that Holy Spirit has a habit of getting my undivided attention while I'm flying home from one of our international schools. This was true when He began to set me on a journey of discovering the unreasonableness of the Father's love. Out of that revelation came the following writing that I call, "I Love You When: A Letter From God."

I have read this letter on several occasions in public settings and have discovered that it challenges people's concepts of God's love. I can see the questions register on their faces as they try to reason out that which is unreasonable. It is my desire to put this letter into an illustrated children's book one day so that young children can start their lives with an accurate understanding of how much God loves them. That way, we may not have to undo in them the same false concepts of His love that we built up in our own minds.

Let me make it clear, I do not believe that God ignores sin or excuses rebellion. Every choice has consequence, every action an effect. We can grieve His Spirit and cause Him sorrow. The good news, however, is that God does not allow our failure to stop Him from loving us. If He loved us when we were sinners, would He stop loving us now that we are redeemed children who sometimes fail? I don't think so. Remember, He "so" loved us. That has not stopped.

As you read through the following letter, I challenge you to open your spirit to the Holy Spirit and receive the revelation He desires to give you. You have a choice: you can read this letter as a document, or you can have a fresh encounter with the love of God.

I Love You When: A Letter From God

I love you always.
I love you when you're happy;
  I love you when you're sad;
I love you when you're laughing;
  I love you when you're crying.
I love you when you win;
  I love you when you lose.
I love you when you're up,
  and I love you when you're down.

I love you when you're good;
  I love you when you're bad.
I love you when you're generous;
  I love you when you're stingy.
I love you when you're right;
  I love you when you're wrong.
I love you when you're innocent;
  I love you when you're guilty.
I love you when you succeed
  and I love you when you fail.

I love you when you pray;
  I love you when you don't.
I love you when you obey;
  I love you when you don't.
I love you when you try;
  I love you when you don't.
I love you when you care
  and I love you when you don't.

I love you when you're kind, gentle, and self-
controlled;
I love you when you're angry, unkind, and out
of control.

I love you in the springtime, summer, winter,
and fall.
I love you in the sunshine,
      and I love you in the rain.

I loved you where you've been,
I love you where you are,
And I'll love you where you're going.

I loved you before you were born;
I love you now,
And I will love you forever.

I love you always,
And always means always.
              —God

Endnotes

1. Online reference, Dictionary.com.
2. Author's rendition of Luke 5:5.
3. Vine, William Edwy. *Vine's Expository Dictionary of New Testament Words*, online resource.

That's what we storytellers do.
We restore order with imagination. We instill
hope again and again.

—Walt Disney in the film, "Saving Mr. Banks"

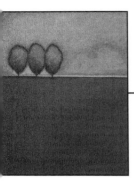

CHAPTER TWELVE

Innocence

Restored

Pamela Travers, better known as P.L. Travers, author and actress, was born Helen Goff on August 9, 1889, in the Australian province of Queensland. Her father, Traverse Goff, was an unsuccessful bank employee and died of influenza after a long battle with alcoholism when Helen was seven years old. Helen's time with her father left such an impression on her young life that it became, in part, the framework for her most famous work, the book *Mary Poppins*.

Mary Poppins became so popular that Walt Disney approached Helen to gain the rights to make the book into a movie. She resisted the idea for many years but

145

finally agreed to sell the rights with the stipulation that she would serve as consultant on the script of the film.

The film, "Saving Mr. Banks," recounts the process of turning the book into what became one of the most successful movies of Disney Studios. "Saving Mr. Banks" draws a connection between Helen's early years with her father, the book's storyline, and the many disagreements between Helen and the Disney scriptwriters.

When we come to Him He reestablishes our innocence and empowers hope.

Though I enjoyed the entire film, I was most captivated by the scene toward the end of the movie where Walt Disney makes one last effort to acquire the rights to the book. He has flown to England where Pamela is living, and he reveals that he is aware of her past which is helping give him a better understanding of her resistance to releasing the script.

In the scene they are sitting in Pamela's very English living room, sipping a "proper" cup of English tea. Walt leans in toward Pamela and shares some of his own childhood story. With this, he assures her that he would produce the film, "Mary Poppins," in a way that would redeem her father's story and then makes the following statement:

> *That's what we storytellers do. We restore order with imagination. We instill hope again and again.*[1]

The Master Storyteller

As I conclude this book, I would suggest that God is the Master Storyteller, restoring order, and in so doing, instilling hope again and again. When we come to Him, He re-establishes our innocence and empowers hope.

When you look at the Scripture's description of Abraham and Sarah in the book of Hebrews, there seems to be a fairly large discrepancy between that account and the history we see recorded in the book of Genesis. In the Old Testament story, we see several lapses in the faith of Abraham and Sarah. Yet, in Hebrews, they are both acclaimed as heroes of faith—Abraham having obeyed God and Sarah having "judged Him faithful who had promised."[2]

What is this all about? Is this just creative storytelling or is something else going on here? I would suggest it is the Master Storyteller at work. And let me make this clear: I believe it is much more than re-telling in order to make a better story. It is redemption. God is a redemptive storyteller, making all things work out for good. This is why Rahab, a harlot from Jericho, is listed with Abraham and Sarah, along with Noah, Moses, Gideon, and others in the heroes Hall of Fame.

Jesus came to seek and save that which is lost. Sin has robed our innocence and stolen our childlikeness. The struggles of life cloud our vision, keeping us from seeing hope's full potential. Fear paralyzes our ability to love and be loved. The weight of responsibility often robs our joy and steals our contentment. Human reasoning diminishes our faith and tempers our wonder. Analysis shrinks our dreams, and caution crimps our sense of adventure. Our passion falls at the feet of our need to be reasonable. These are all symptoms of lost innocence.

When we are born again, our story is retold through the lens of redemption, our innocence is restored, and hope is reborn.

A Redeemed IRS Agent

Growing up in the church, the story of Zacchaeus was not only told quite often, but it was also recounted in song. Therefore, this man's story should be familiar to anyone who, like me, was a prenatal church attendee. Even so, let me retell it here and reveal something you may not have noticed before.

"Zacchaeus" is a Jewish name, so we know that by birth, he was a Jew. He was also a Roman tax collector, and as such he was not seen as a true Hebrew by his fellow Jews of the day. His less-than-honorable Roman occupation left him an outcast from the proper Hebrew culture.

Then comes Jesus into the picture. He invites himself to Zacchaeus' house for dinner, and His very presence results in the repentance of Zacchaeus with a promise of full restitution.

Jesus' response to him is rather startling: "Salvation has come to this home today, for this man has shown himself to be a true son of Abraham."[23]

Did you catch what Jesus did? In calling him a true "son of Abraham" Jesus restored the innocence of Zacchaeus, returning him to his true identity as a man of God's chosen people.

Jesus then makes a statement that summarizes his treatment of Zacchaeus and capsulizes His true mission:

148

For the Son of Man has come to seek and save that which is lost (v. 10).

An Invitation and a Promise

Jesus gave the disciples the instruction that in order to enter the Kingdom of God we must come "as a little child."[4] I believe that this instruction is both an invitation and a promise. It is an invitation into an intimate relationship with God through childlike faith. And since we lost our childlike innocence through sin, it is also a promise to restore that which is lost: lost hope, lost dreams, lost passion, lost wonder, lost love, lost innocence.

God never requires what He does not empower. If He requires that we come as a child, His promise to restore childlikeness must be resident in His requirement. God made this possible through Jesus:

> *For He made Him who knew no sin to be sin for us, that we might become the righteousness of God in Him* (2 Corinthians 5:21).

Paul, in writing to the Ephesian church paints a descriptive picture of our redemption:

> *And you, He made alive, who were dead in trespasses and sins... we all once conducted ourselves in the lusts of our flesh, fulfilling the desires of the flesh and of the mind, and were by nature children of wrath... But God, who is rich in mercy, because of His great love with which He loved us, even when we were dead in trespasses, made us alive together with*

Christ... and raised us up together, and made us sit in the heavenly places in Christ Jesus (Ephesians 2:1-6).

This is good news to anyone reading this book. The Master Storyteller wants to rewrite—redeem—your story and instill hope again. He sent Jesus to bring back your childlike innocence so that you can respond to Him in faith, unbound by human reason.

The great Author and Finisher of our faith is waiting to renew our childlike sense of wonder and adventure. He is present with us right now to reestablish our permission to dream again like a child with an innocent imagination.

That's what we storytellers do. We restore order with imagination. We instill hope again and again.

You are now at the end of this book and at the beginning of your journey as a prisoner of hope. My prayer for you is simply this:

May God so captivate you with His love and a spirit of expectation that you will adventure into the future with your heart freshly tuned to the life-giving sound of hope.

Endnotes

1. "Saving Mr. Banks," film produced by Walt Disney Studios, 2013.
2. Hebrews 11:11.
3. Based on Luke 19:9.
4. See Mark 10:15.

About the Author

David Crone and his wife Deborah are the senior leaders of a community of believers called The Mission in Vacaville, California. They have been in full-time vocational ministry for over 40 years and have served at The Mission for over 20 years. While at The Mission, they helped transition a local church into a global ministry that provides resources for their region and the nations. Their value for team ministry has developed a culture of strong leaders, some of who serve with David and Deborah on the core leadership team of The Mission. Their lives and ministry are known for authenticity, a passion for God's presence, and a pursuit of His kingdom on Earth.

David is a director of Mission School of the Supernatural, a ministry of The Mission, and, along with Deborah, serves on the teaching staff of the school. They also are part of the Global Legacy apostolic team that oversees a growing number of churches in partnership for revival.

In partnership with The Mission, Mark 16:15 International, and Kingdom Development Group of Australia, David has developed supernatural training schools in the Philippines and Fiji. These schools train believers in releasing Heaven on Earth through personal transformation and signs and wonders. He serves as the International Director of Mission Fiji and Deeper Life, Philippines.

PRISONER OF HOPE

David has traveled extensively, ministering in 23 nations. He is also the author of four books. His wife, Deborah, an accomplished artist, has her paintings in the gallery of one of the largest art cultures in the world, Maui, Hawaii. David and Deborah are welcomed speakers at conferences and churches, both at home and abroad.

Other Books by

David Crone

Declarations That Empower Us

Foreword by Kris Vallotton

In *Declarations That Empower Us*, David Crone shares a multitude of Holy Spirit-inspired proclamations and speaks to the empowering quality of coming into agreement with Heaven through the act of declaration. This book is more than a teaching manuscript or anecdotal journal; it is a resource manual for those looking for language to express their resolve in critical moments along their journey.   (143 pages)

Decisions That Define Us

Foreword by Bill Johnson

In *Decisions That Define Us*, David Crone documents his personal and corporate journey of transformation as senior leader of a transitioning church in Northern California. Each decision in this book represents the spoils of a battle fought and costly Kingdom lessons learned by this leader, his team, and their local fellowship. Within the pages of this book, you will be challenged and inspired to pursue God's Kingdom at any cost and to discover practical ways to expressing the supernatural in your own life.   (130 pages)

The Power of Your Life Message
Foreword by Bill Johnson

Author David Crone shares his deeply personal journey which brought him into an intimate relationship with His heavenly Father. You will be challenged to change your mindset, which then opens the door to internal transformation. You will learn how to define your life message and how to make decisions that lead to fulfilling God's exhilarating and exciting plans for your current and eternal destiny. (236 pages)

For more resources from
David Crone, visit
The Mission Bookstore
online at:

store.iMissionChurch.com

Also available at:

Amazon.com
DaveCrone.com

Fine Art by Deborah Crone

Deborah Crone's art can be found at Sargent's Fine Art Gallery in Lahaina, Maui, and at her gallery in Vacaville, California.

More of her art expressions can be viewed online at:
> nisart.net

For inquiries and more information, contact Deborah at:
> deborahnis@sbcglobal.net

To learn more about the
ministries of David and
Deborah Crone, or request
them for speaking at your
church or conference, contact
by email:
dcrone@iMissionChurch.com

Made in the USA
Charleston, SC
12 July 2015